Communications
in Computer and Information Science   1471

More information about this series at https://link.springer.com/bookseries/7899

Alvaro David Orjuela-Cañón · Jesus A. Lopez ·
Julián David Arias-Londoño ·
Juan Carlos Figueroa-García (Eds.)

Applications of Computational Intelligence

4th IEEE Colombian Conference, ColCACI 2021
Virtual Event, May 27–28, 2021
Revised Selected Papers

 Springer

Editors
Alvaro David Orjuela-Cañón ⓘ
Universidad del Rosario
Bogotá, Colombia

Jesus A. Lopez ⓘ
Universidad Autónoma de Occidente
Cali, Colombia

Julián David Arias-Londoño ⓘ
University of Antioquia
Medellín, Colombia

Juan Carlos Figueroa-García ⓘ
Universidad Distrital Francisco José de
Caldas
Bogotá, Colombia

ISSN 1865-0929   ISSN 1865-0937 (electronic)
Communications in Computer and Information Science
ISBN 978-3-030-91307-6   ISBN 978-3-030-91308-3 (eBook)
https://doi.org/10.1007/978-3-030-91308-3

This Springer imprint is published by the registered company Springer Nature Switzerland AG
The registered company address is: Gewerbestrasse 11, 6330 Cham, Switzerland

Preface

The computational intelligence (CI) area is increasingly employed in engineering problems of the Latin America (LA) region. LA scientists have focused their efforts into the CI field as a way to deal with problems of interest for the international community but also of great impact in the LA region. Many different areas including optimization of energy and transportation systems, computer-aided medical diagnoses, bioinformatics, mining of massive data sets, robotics, and automatic surveillance systems, among many others, are commonly addressed problems from this part of the world because of the great potential such applications could have in developing countries.

The world has been living through hard times, the difficult situation due to the COVID-19 pandemic has changed humanity and our different interactions. This year, 2021, has been a transition year, moving out of the pandemic crisis. Slowly, the world has returned to normal life, mainly because of the massive vaccination programs. As mentioned, our methods of communicating have transformed, challenging us to provide new opportunities to accomplish academic activities, such as conferences, publication, and generation of more scientific material.

The IEEE Colombian Conference on Computational Intelligence (IEEE ColCACI) knows this difficult task, trying to contribute to the field of CI in these uncertain times. The first and second editions of the conference were held in person. Due the pandemic situation, the third (2020) edition of ColCACI was developed in a virtual mode, opening the possibility to hybrid conferences (a mixture of participants in person and online) in the future, motivating and divulgating the advances in the area, and introducing more attractive options for participation in the coming years. The IEEE ColCACI 2021 conference was held in virtual mode, aiming to support the development of academic activities and promote the impact of computational intelligence in Colombia, the Andean region, and Latin America, with the hope that the situation gets better to allow in-person meetings in future editions.

As a result of the COVID-19 pandemic, in 2020 and 2021 the number of proposals that sought to answer questions related to problems that can be solved with the application of artificial intelligence (AI), bringing wellness for humanity, increased. This approach is named artificial intelligence for social good (AI2SG). It is worth mentioning that the computational intelligence (CI) area is increasingly employed in solving problems with social impact in the Latin America (LA) region. Some of the papers that were presented at ColCACI 2021 included AI applications for mobile devices, computer-aided medical diagnoses, traffic control solutions, and modeling of extreme climate events, among many others. Because of the great potential and high impact of AI2SG in developing countries, we expect that, in the future, ColCACI will be a conference where researchers and practitioners of AI in Colombia and Latin America can share applications to solve common problems in our countries.

In its virtual fourth edition, the IEEE Colombian Conference on Computational Intelligence (IEEE ColCACI 2021) was fortified with contributions from scientists, engineers, and practitioners working on applications and theory of CI techniques. We received 22 papers by authors from three Andean countries and selected 12 papers for oral presentation in virtual mode due to the COVID-19 pandemic. In this way, the conference still provided an international forum for CI researchers and practitioners to share their more recent advances and results. This post-proceedings contains revised and selected papers from ColCACI 2021, including extended versions of the seven best papers presented at the conference. We will continue working to offer more excellent IEEE ColCACI programs in the future.

Finally, we would like to thank the IEEE Colombia Section, the IEEE Computational Intelligence Colombian Chapter, the IEEE Computational Intelligence Society, the Universidad Autónoma de Occidente, the Universidad del Rosario, the Universidad Distrital Francisco Jose de Caldas, the Universidad de Antioquia, and Springer for their support. Also, special thanks go to all volunteers, participants, and the whole crew that worked together to make a successful conference. See you at IEEE ColCACI 2022!

November 2021

Alvaro David Orjuela-Cañón
Julián David Arias-Londoño
Jesus A. Lopez
Juan Carlos Figueroa-García

Organization

General Co-chairs

Jesús Alfonso López Sotelo   Universidad Autónoma de Occidente, Colombia
Alvaro David Orjuela-Cañón   Universidad del Rosario, Colombia

Program Committee Chairs

Julián David Arias-Londoño   Universidad de Antioquia, Colombia
Juan Carlos Figueroa-García   Universidad Distrital Francisco José de Caldas,
     · Colombia

Publication Chairs

Alvaro David Orjuela-Cañón   Universidad del Rosario, Colombia
Diana Briceño   Universidad Distrital Francisco José de Caldas,
     Colombia

Financial Chair

José David Cely   Universidad Distrital Francisco José de Caldas,
     Colombia

Webmaster

Fabian Martinez   IEEE Colombia, Colombia

Program Committee

Alvaro David Orjuela-Cañón   Universidad del Rosario, Colombia
Jesús Alfonso López Sotelo   Universidad Autónoma de Occidente, Colombia
Julián David Arias-Londoño   Universidad de Antioquia, Colombia
Juan Carlos Figueroa-García   Universidad Distrital Francisco José de Caldas,
     Colombia
Danton Ferreira   Universidade Federal de Lavras, Brazil
Efren Gorrostieta   Universidad Autónoma de Queretaro, Mexico
Cristian Rodríguez Rivero   University of California, Davis, USA
Jose Alfredo Costa   Universidade Federal do Rio Grande do Norte,
     Brazil

Contents

Biomedical Applications

Anemia Detection Using a Full Embedded Mobile Application with YOLO Algorithm

Maileth Rivero-Palacio⑩, Wilfredo Alfonso-Morales$^{(✉)}$⑩,
and Eduardo Caicedo-Bravo⑩

School of Electrical and Electronic Engineering, Universidad del Valle,
Santiago de Cali, Colombia
{maileth.rivero,wilfredo.alfonso,eduardo.caicedo}@correounivalle.edu.co

Abstract. This paper proposes the development of a mobile application
for anemia detection using YOLO v5. The app aims to support healthcare professionals in identifying anemia in children in places where mobile
signals are missing (isolated). We used an image dataset obtained from
Universidad Peruana Cayetano Heredia, which contains pictures of children under five years old and their prognosis by the blood test. Although
YOLO v5 gets good results using a computer, its implementation in a
mobile app reduces its performance. Despite this, the app shows a sensitivity of 0.71 and a specificity of 0.89 to detect anemia.

Keywords: Anemia · Mobile app · YOLO · Deep learning

1 Introduction

Anemia is a disease that, according to a study made by the World Health
Organization (WHO), affects approximately 2 billion people, mostly residents
of developing countries, children under five years of age, pregnant women, and
the elderly [20]. Anemia can arise, among other causes, due to iron deficiency
in food, hereditary or genetic factors, or hemorrhages. The most distinctive, as
it progresses, symptoms are weakness, tiredness, delays in mental and physical development, dizziness, headache, pale lips, eyes and nails, and even lack
of appetite [17,20]. There are different methods for diagnosing anemia: conventional methods, which primarily use clinical blood tests; and non-conventional
methods, which use computational techniques such as Deep Learning to analyze images of blood and specific body parts such as fingernails, tongue, and
conjunctiva [1,2,20].

Due to the need to identify anemia early, in order to mitigate its effects, different institutions have taken advantage of the increase in processing capabilities
to develop mobile applications that use non-conventional techniques. Healthcare
personnel takes images from a cell phone camera to send them to a server that
processes them and provides a diagnosis [13,22]. Although the systems developed

A. D. Orjuela-Cañón et al. (Eds.): ColCACI 2021, CCIS 1471, pp. 3–17, 2022.
https://doi.org/10.1007/978-3-030-91308-3_1

perform reliable anemia diagnoses, their use is limited in Internet access areas, as all processing must be done on a server. Currently, cellular technologies are more affordable for users and have sufficient modules to capture images, send data, and process information. Together with new tools, both have enabled the development of more complex mobile applications that can be used by the user once installed on the mobile and that rarely require an Internet connection.

This paper proposes developing an embedded mobile application using a deep learning technique to support healthcare personnel in diagnosing anemia in isolated locations or populations that do not have the resources, Internet access, or a clinical laboratory to analyze the tests. The document is organized as follows: Section 2 presents some work developed for the unconventional diagnosis of anemia. Section 3 describes the techniques used to develop the model implemented in the application and the concepts used in its evaluation. The procedure executed to obtain the model and the development of the application is described in Sect. 4. Section 5 presents the results obtained from both the implemented architecture and the mobile application. The last section presents the general conclusions and the future directions of the work.

2   Related Works

Due to the great potential of deep neural networks in several applications, they have also been widely used to detect different diseases. YOLO (You Only Look Once) is a kind of these architecture used for that purpose. In [25] authors used YOLO v3 into a deep learning system called BMSNet to help in the interpretation of bone marrow smear and for the diagnosis of hematological diseases. The model contained a feature extraction architecture based on SE-ResNet, a pyramidal feature network, and the bounding box prediction subnetwork based on YOLO v3. They selected 42 bone marrow smears from patients with a variety of diagnoses as leukemia, myelodysplastic syndrome (MDS), myeloproliferative disease (MPD), multiple myeloma (MM), aplastic anemia (AA), and lymphoma without bone marrow involvement for cell lineage collections. They used a 1000x microscope and camera to manually capture a total of 291 (1920×2048) high-resolution pictures, which were labeled in eight categories: erythroid, blasts, myeloid, lymphoid, plasma cells, monocytes, megakaryocytes, and unable to identify. They also used a 6-fold cross-validation process to evaluate model performance by getting an average accuracy of the bounding box of 67.4%, with an accuracy and sensitivity in the diagnosis similar to the specialist evaluation. The results obtained in this work confirm the potential of deep neural network architectures, especially YOLO, to detect diseases. The updated version of YOLO (version 5) uses the CSPNet backbone and has demonstrated higher accuracy of results and even better inference capabilities compared to previous versions [12].

Furthermore, other architectures have also been used to detect diseases such as Parkinson [19], skin cancer [7], and anemia [4]. In anemia, different computational techniques have been used based on blood or body color analysis. Among the blood color analysis, [1,11] used a digital camera to capture images and implemented feedforward networks to detect anemia. In [1], they compared the results with those provided by a laboratory test, obtaining a match of 85%. While in [11], they evaluated the model on 16 blood samples obtaining a specificity of 82% and a sensitivity of 83%.

On the other hand, researchers usually take ocular conjunctiva and nail bed pictures through digital cameras to be processed using machine learning algorithms for body color analysis. The first group includes [4,5], where the ocular conjunctiva is analyzed. In [4], they developed two algorithms for populations with a high incidence of anemia, based on features in HSI and RGB color spaces, and another for low incidence, based on color textures. The quick algorithm obtained a sensitivity of 62% and a specificity of 53% using two color-based features. The robust algorithm used all features, followed by the use of a classifier, either artificial neural network (ANN) or support vector machine (SVM), obtaining a sensitivity of 75% and a specificity of 58% for ANN and a sensitivity of 78% and a specificity of 61% for SVM. In [5], the authors also got images from a cell phone; for the features, they calculated the erythema index and defined a threshold to determine anemia, obtaining a sensitivity of 57% (74%) and a specificity of 83% (71%) with the digital camera (cell phone camera).

Regarding applications for anemia diagnosis, many of them use cellphones to send information to a server which gets a result using classification algorithms [6,13,21]. In [13], a mobile application captures images from the nail beds and sends them to a server that compares the pallor of the nails with image templates. The results were compared with the evaluation of specialists, outperforming the latter. In [6], after applying image segmentation, a server uses a convolutional network that analyzes and provides a result; the results were compared with those of a laboratory test, obtaining a sensitivity of 77.58%. Finally, besides palpebral conjunctival images, in [21] used tongue images to determine anemia. They compared their results with the laboratory tests, obtaining a sensitivity of 91.89% and specificity of 85.18% using the tongue images and sensitivity of 91.89% and specificity of 79.34% for the conjunctiva images.

Although previous studies demonstrated that reliable inference could be made using the mobile application as a link to server processing, other applications are practical for implementing models directly on cellphones such as *Pytorch* and *YOLO*. Even with their limited processing capabilities, an embedded mobile application would help diagnose populations without medical or technological resources for earlier anemia diagnosis than traditional blood tests [23].

3 Theoretical Framework

3.1 YOLO V5

YOLO v5 is an architecture (see Fig. 1) specially designed for object detection in images or videos. The architecture consists of three main blocks presented below [3,18]:

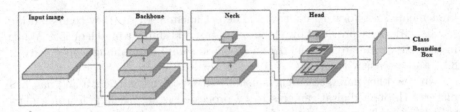

Fig. 1. YOLO architecture. Taken from [3]

- **Backbone**: It is a convolutional neural network that extracts features from the input image. In YOLO v5, CSPNet is used as a backbone. CSPNet is a strategy that partitions the base layer feature map into two parts and then merges them through an inter-stage hierarchy. During the development of CSPNet it was found that excessive inference calculations were mainly due to the duplication of gradient information within the network optimization, so in CSPNet it was decided to avoid duplication of gradient information by truncating its flow. The feature map is divided into two parts, one part performs a convolution operation and the other concatenates the convolution result of the previous layer. Due to the reduction of gradient information this backbone allows to reduce memory cost, bottlenecks, parameters and floating point operations per second, since the amount of computation is evenly distributed in each layer of the convolutional network [24].
- **Neck:** Consists of several layers responsible for grouping image features into pyramids, improving the generalization in the scaling of objects in the model. This block seeks to improve the identification of objects at different scales and sizes. Yolo v5 implements PANet (Path Aggregation Network for Instance Segmentation) to drive the flow of information. PANet adopts a new feature pyramid network (FPN) structure with an enhanced upstream path, which improves the propagation of low-level features. At the same time, adaptive feature clustering, which links the feature network and all feature levels, is used to make useful information from each feature level propagate directly to the next subnetwork. The Neck improves the utilization of accurate location signals in the lower layers and thus the accuracy of object location.
- **Head:** Takes the features generated by the *Neck* and performs the prediction by determining the class to which the object belongs and the bounding box. The Head generates three different feature map sizes (18×18, 36×36, 72×72) to predict the small, medium and large objects.

3.2   Performance Verification

Performance metrics derived from the confusion matrix such as accuracy, sensitivity, and specificity are used to evaluate the neural network model. The matrix represents the data distribution regarding the classes obtained in each experiment with respect to the real classes. The nomenclature of the matrix is:

- *TP*: *true positives*. Anemia correctly detected.

- *FP*: *false positives.* Type I error.
- *TN*: *true negatives.* Non-anemia correctly detected.
- *FN*: *false negatives.* Type II error.

Accuracy is the percentage of correct predictions of the model, i.e., the number of correct predictions out of the total input data. It is a metric that should not be fully relied upon when dealing with unbalanced classes; as a result, it could be biased towards the majority class. Equation (1) calculates the Accuracy.

$$Accuracy = \frac{TP + TN}{TP + TN + FP + FN} \tag{1}$$

Recall or Sensitivity reports the number of true positives correctly identified out of the existing total. The higher the *recall*, the more positive samples the model has correctly classified. The calculation of *recall* is done by the Eq. (2).

$$Recall = \frac{TP}{TP + FN} \tag{2}$$

Specificity is also called the true negative rate. It detects true negative cases that were predicted to be negative (or true negative). A higher specificity means that more healthy people will be appropriately diagnosed. It is calculated by the Eq. (3).

$$Specificity = \frac{TN}{TN + FP} \tag{3}$$

3.3   Metrics for Measuring Bounding-Box

The mAP (*mean Average Precision*) is a metric frequently used to measure the accuracy of object detections. It allows evaluating if the object class is correct and if the bounding box position is good. It compares the real bounding box with the detected one by returning a value that varies between 0 and 1. A value close to 1 means a well-detected box concerning the real one.

4   Materials and Methods

4.1   Dataset: Acquisition and Debugging

Initially, there are 1012 images of 3120×4160 pixels, provided by the Universidad Peruana Cayetano Heredia (UPCH). The set of images is private and was acquired in a health brigade carried out by specialists from the *UPCH* in rural areas of difficult access in order to develop a mobile application that would help in the diagnosis of anemia in children under 5 years of age. As the images handled here are biometric data, it was necessary to have the authorization of each of the patients' relatives beforehand for their manipulation and processing. No standard procedures were used to capture the images, i.e., the pictures were taken under different lighting and occlusion conditions. They only tried to ensure that a color pattern appeared in all the images, which would be used later for their processing.

Due to images were blurred and others did not correspond to a child's conjunctiva, we performed a data cleaning procedure to select the most suitable images. The images selected for the final dataset had to meet the following requirements:

– The images had to be in focus; they could not be blurred.
– The images had to contain the conjunctiva of the child.
– The images should be able to distinguish the color of the conjunctiva and the blood vessels.
– No tabs covering the conjunctiva could appear on the image.
– Each image had to have the child's Hb (hemoglobin concentration) value associated with it.

Finally, we retained 457 images, 121 to the Anemia class and 336 to the non-anemia class.

4.2 Image Pre-processing

In order to reduce processing time and computational effort and improve the system's accuracy, we cropped the image to 1600 × 1600 pixels around the conjunctiva. The cropping was done by applying region segmentation of the conjunctiva and the pixels around. The regions segmentation were divided according to color to locate the conjunctiva area. Initially, the image is read in RGB color space and turned to HSV; a *medianblur* filter is applied to the H channel to remove noise. Otsu's binarization is applied, the image is converted to black and white and morphological operations (closing and dilation) are used to improve the segmentation mask. The pixel with the highest value is defined employing the histogram calculation to crop the image from this point.

4.3 Data Augmentation and Labeling

With an unbalanced dataset (Anemia class was lower than the Non-Anemia class), we decided to apply data augmentation to the Anemia class. Data augmentation is a technique applied to datasets to equalize the number of images of all classes, reduce overfitting, and improve the accuracy and generalization of the results [15]. For the generation of new images, the existing ones were slightly modified by applying flipping and rotation. The data augmentation was performed using the Robloflow platform, which allows uploading up to 1000 images in its free version, pre-processing and obtaining the generated images by direct download or a *link* usable in any processing platform such as *Google Colaboratory*.

The next step was to label the images according to the class (Non-Anemia and Anemia). Here, we used information provided by UPCH to classify the images based on the table of hemoglobin concentrations. With the Hb value and the levels registered in the table for children under five years of age, it was possible to define the class to which each image corresponded.

The images were labeled using CVAT[1] (*Computer Vision Annotation Tool*), an intuitive open-source tool, executable in web browsers, that requires no installation and allows labeling images and videos, in *json* or other formats. The tagging information is stored in a *json* file, which presents in its structure: image name, size, class, and coordinates in pixels of each region (upper left and lower right corner).

4.4 Sets of Data

The total images were divided into three sets: training, validation, and test. Each of the images in these sets serves a specific function. The training set allows to adjust the neural network weights; the validation set brings a way to evaluate the network's performance during training, mainly to avoid overfitting; the test set is used to evaluate the performance of the obtained model.

Since the dataset is relatively small, considering other applications where the image datasets are considerable [14], the sets were divided into 10% for *testing*, 10% for *validation* and 80% for *training* similarly to [16]. The division was done through the *Roboflow* platform, which allows downloading an executable *link* in *Google Colaboratory* with which the dataset is loaded much faster. Thus, we got 539 training images and 66 images for each validation and test set.

4.5 Training

For the training of YOLO v5, we followed the steps of the *GitHub*[2] created by *Ultralitycs*. The network was cloned and used in *Google Colaboratory* from the *GitHub* repository taking into account the necessary dependencies and libraries; the dataset was exported via the *link* provided by *Roboflow*. First, the neural network was tested with the default configuration; it presented good results; therefore, it was re-trained with the same configuration. Only the image size was slightly increased while the threshold and the number of epochs were adjusted. The visualization was performed through *TensorBoard*, a tool of *Google Collaboratory*. All metrics were derived from the confusion matrix, such as accuracy, sensitivity, and specificity (see Table 1).

In addition, taking advantage of the potential of *transfer learning*, a pre-trained model was used to process the information. Among the advantages of using *transfer learning*, the reduction of training time and its maximization in performance stand out. During training, the use of *GPUs* and *TPUs* environments offered by the *Google Colaboratory* cloud service was taken advantage of;

---

[1] https://cvat.org/.

[2] https://github.com/ultralytics/yolov5.

this environment allows working in *Python* and has *machine learning* and artificial vision libraries. *Google Colaboratory* is offering a Tesla K80 graphics card, 12 GB of RAM and 330 GB of storage for free, and about 12 h of free usage time.

The pre-trained model was re-trained using RGB images since the synaptic weights of these pre-trained networks are not adjusted in the training process; indeed, they are dedicated only to the refinement of the last layers. One advantage of using a deep neural network is that pre-processing techniques for illumination, contrast, or occlusion are unnecessary. A deep neural network provides in the inner layers a set of enriched features that are processed by other stages of the proposed architecture [8].

4.6   Mobile Application Design

The Rational Unified Process (RUP) methodology was used to build the application, which allows knowing the needs of the system in order to make it functional [10]. Thus, the functional and non-functional requirements were initially defined, one for the neural network and the other for the application. These are presented below.

Functional and Non-functional Requirements define the hardware and software specifications to be met by the system to be developed and used, respectively. Both requirements can be categorized as essential (E) or optional (O) to achieve the goals. They were divided into neural network functional requirements and application functional requirements.

The neural network requirements include everything relevant to the development of the model, from the loading of the neural network to the conversion to the PyTorch script of the best-trained model. The application requirements include the main functionalities of the application.

The functional requirements of the neural network:

- Import Yolo v5 architecture and install dependencies (E).
- Import images and dataset labels from Roboflow (E).
- Configure the neural network (E).
- Train the neural network with the pre-processed images (E).
- Visualize the training results in Tensorboard (O).
- Do inference on the images of the test dataset (E).
- Verify the performance of the trained network through the confusion matrix and other evaluation metrics (E).
- Convert the model obtained in the prediction to PytorchScript (E).

The functional requirements of the application:

- Allow user to choose between predicting image or saving personal information to the cell phone (E).

- Allow the user to choose between predicting an image in the device's gallery or a captured image and making the prediction (E).
- Allow the user to save his personal information (E).
- Display the image to predict the class and the score obtained (E).
- Allow the user to save the resulting image in the phone (E).
- Incorporate the model trained in Pytorch in the application (E).

Between the non-functional requirements we have:

- This project will be developed in Pytorch v3.6.8 (E).
- This project will use Pytorch (E).
- This project will use Flutter SDK (E).
- This project will use Adobe XD (O).
- This project will use Google Colaboratory (O).
- This project will use Android Studio (O).

The use cases were also defined, which allow identifying and dividing the functionality of the system. It describes the sequence of iterations between the system actor or interactor and the system. Fourteen use cases were defined, one per requirement: import the neural network architecture and install dependencies, import images and labels, configure the neural network architecture, train the neural network, visualize the training results in Tensorboard, make the inference, verify the performance of the trained network, convert the model to PyTorch Script, choose the initial options, choose the image and make a prediction, save personal information, show prediction result, save prediction and incorporate the model.

In response to system requirements, the application's *Mockup* was designed using *Adobe XD*[3] software, which allows the creation of physical designs of mobile applications and usability tests due to its medium-high level of detail. The programming was done through the *Dart*[4] language, using the *framework Flutter*[5] and *Android Studio*[6].

The application does not require data or internet resources, but it will use hardware resources. It is a hybrid application since it uses native functions of *Android* and *plugins* of *Flutter* to have access to the application functionalities. It was necessary to create a *plugin* to connect the native functionalities of *Android* with *Flutter* and make the inference process. In the native part of *Android*, dependencies of *pytorch_android* and *pytorch_ android_torchvision* were installed, which allow importing the modules and functions necessary to perform the inference. The application was tested in the *Android Studio* emulator with a *Pixel 3a XL API 30* device *(Android 9)* and the *Samsung A20* cell phone with *Android 10*.

---

[3] https://www.adobe.com/products/xd.html.
[4] https://dart.dev/.
[5] https://flutter.dev/.
[6] https://developer.android.com/.

4.7   Model Incorporation

The incorporation of the YOLO v5 model into the application was performed through Torch Script, which is a subset of *Python* which, although not all the features of *Python* work, provides enough functionality to compute tensors and make a portable implementation. After embedding, a *assets* folder is generated in the application for the model as well as a *.txt* file with the classes' names. Once the image is captured or selected from the gallery, it is analyzed to define its class. Finally, the screen displays the image with its bounding box, class, and the obtained score.

5   Results and Analysis

5.1   YOLO V5

Two scenarios were performed with the architecture: with and without cropping pre-processing stage.

Yolo, with Pre-processing Stage, takes the image cropped at 1600×1600 around the conjunctiva and performs data augmentation (cropping by 30%) to obtain more images in the training set. The process resulted in 1617 total images in the training set. Figure 2 presents the confusion matrix obtained with the test set. The performance verification shows precision and recall of 0.91, the sensitivity of 0.86, and specificity of 0.95.

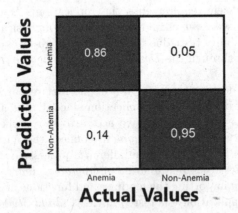

Fig. 2. Yolo confusion matrix with pre-processing

Yolo, Without Pre-processing Stage, allows verifying the ability of YOLO v5 to distinguish conjunctiva and detect anemia in an image without cropping. Figure 3 shows results of the prediction, where regardless of the conjunctiva location, even rotated, the model can correctly detect the class and locate the conjunctiva.

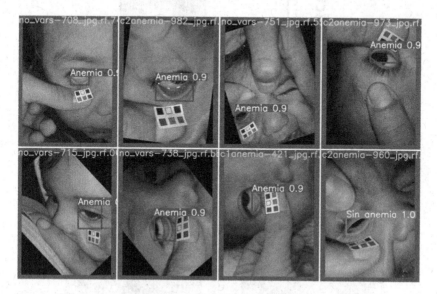

Fig. 3. Prediction result with Yolo without pre-processing. Blue labels: Anemia. Orange labels: Non-Anemia. (Color figure online)

The matrix in Fig. 4, compared to the previous model, shows an increase in true positives (anemia). This last aspect is of great importance since it improves the prognosis of anemia, i.e., improves the sensitivity since it reduces the false-negative rate. The performance results obtain an accuracy of 0.93, recall and sensitivity of 0.91, and specificity of 0.95.

5.2   Mobile Application

The ability to correctly predict anemia and each functional requirement was tested in the mobile application. These were performed on a *SAMSUNG A20* phone with 3GB RAM and 1.6GHz *Exynos 7884 Octa-Core* processor using images from the test set. Figure 5 shows the prediction result on the mobile device achieving a sensitivity of 0.71 and specificity of 0.89.

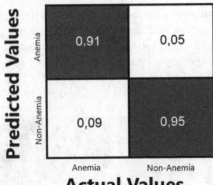

Fig. 4. Yolo confusion matrix with no pre-processing

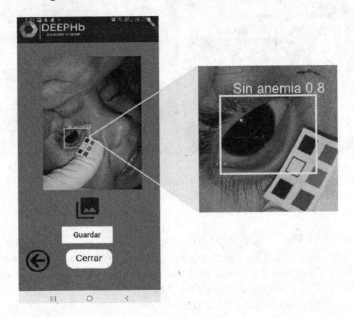

Fig. 5. Application prediction

The confusion matrix for the mobile application is presented in Fig. 6; the comparative results between PC and Mobile YOLO implementation are summarized in Table 1.

In addition to evaluating the system's ability to predict anemia correctly, the tests also evaluated the storage of patient data and the other functionalities of an application, such as switching from one interface to another; operation of the buttons, the camera, access to the gallery and the phone directories.

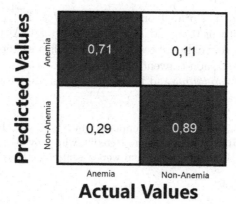

Fig. 6. Confusion matrix of the prediction tests using the mobile application in *SAM-SUNG A20*

Table 1. Prediction test results

Evaluation metrics	Result YOLO/PC	Result YOLO/Mobile
Accuracy	0.93	0.80
Sensitivity	0.91	0.71
Specificity	0.95	0.89
mAP	0.95	0.79

Although the value of the metrics has been reduced, the detection system shows good results. The reduction of the values is because the model in the mobile application suffers a binary reduction of processing when it is converted to TorchScript. In the conversion process, multiple operations and roundings are performed on the results, which reduces the accuracy of the inference, and an optimization process is done where 32-bit floats are converted to 8-bits so that the models can be implemented in embedded devices with lower storage capacities [9]. Adjusting the model parameters over mobile devices with higher image processing capabilities for better feature extraction could provide better results.

6 Conclusions

The application developed in this work demonstrates that neural networks are a helpful tool for diagnosing anemia and can be embedded into a mobile application. It improves the outlook for anemia diagnosis in remote areas that do not have laboratory equipment or specialists to perform a test. This system is independent of Internet access to process conjunctiva images and detect anemia by providing an image with the bounding box, the detected class, and the obtained score.

Several tests were performed on the *SAMSUNG A20* phone application, obtaining a sensitivity of 0.71 and a specificity of 0.89. Although it does not exceed the results of conventional tests, it is a significant step to detect anemia in isolated places, using non-conventional methods of diagnosis. Applying techniques such as *cross-validation* and better parameter tuning could yield results very similar to laboratory tests.

Acknowledgments. This work was supported by Professor Mirko Zimic and his team from Universidad Peruana Cayetano Heredia, who provided the images with the hemoglobin concentrations of each one and were essential in the training of the neural network models.

References

1. Anantharaman, R., Velazquez, M., Lee, Y.: Utilizing mask R-CNN for detection and segmentation of oral diseases. In: 2018 IEEE International Conference on Bioinformatics and Biomedicine (BIBM). IEEE, December 2018. https://doi.org/10.1109/bibm.2018.8621112
2. Anomym: Anemia Detection Methods in Low-Resource Settings: A Manual For Health Workers. Pagina web, December 1997. https://path.azureedge.net/media/documents/TS_anemia_guide_health_workers.pdf
3. Bochkovskiy, A., Wang, C.Y., Liao, H.Y.M.: YOLOv4: optimal speed and accuracy of object detection. ArXiv, April 2020
4. Chen, Y.M., Miaou, S.G., Bian, H.: Examining palpebral conjunctiva for anemia assessment with image processing methods. Comput. Methods Programs Biomed. **137**, 125–135 (2016). https://doi.org/10.1016/j.cmpb.2016.08.025
5. Collings, S., Thompson, O., Hirst, E., Goossens, L., George, A., Weinkove, R.: Non-invasive detection of anaemia using digital photographs of the conjunctiva. PLOS ONE **11**(4), e0153286 (2016). https://doi.org/10.1371/journal.pone.0153286
6. Delgado-Rivera, G., et al.: Method for the automatic segmentation of the palpebral conjunctiva using image processing. In: 2018 IEEE International Conference on Automation/XXIII Congress of the Chilean Association of Automatic Control (ICA-ACCA). IEEE, October 2018. https://doi.org/10.1109/ica-acca.2018.8609744
7. Esteva, A., et al.: Dermatologist-level classification of skin cancer with deep neural networks. Nature **542**(7639), 115–118, January 2017. https://doi.org/10.1038/nature21056
8. Goodfellow, I., Bengio, Y., Courville, A.: Deep Learning. MIT Press (2016). http://www.deeplearningbook.org
9. Ibrahim, M.: Pytorch vs Tensorflow 2021. Web Page, May 2021. https://towardsdatascience.com/pytorch-vs-tensorflow-2021-d403504d7bc3
10. Kruchten, P.: The Rational Unified Process: An Introduction. Addison-Wesley Professional (2004)
11. Kumar, M.R., Mahadevappa, M., Goswami, D.: Low cost point of care estimation of Hemoglobin levels. In: 2014 International Conference on Medical Imaging, m-Health and Emerging Communication Systems (MedCom). IEEE, November 2014. https://doi.org/10.1109/medcom.2014.7006007
12. Maithani, M.: Guide to Yolov5 for real-time object detection. Web Page (2020). https://analyticsindiamag.com/yolov5/

13. Mannino, R.G., et al.: Smartphone app for non-invasive detection of anemia using only patient-sourced photos. Nat. Commun. **9**(1) (2018). https://doi.org/10.1038/s41467-018-07262-2

14. Mubarok, A.F.A., Dominique, J.A.M., Thias, A.H.: Pneumonia detection with deep convolutional architecture. In: 2019 International Conference of Artificial Intelligence and Information Technology (ICAIIT). IEEE, March 2019. https://doi.org/10.1109/icaiit.2019.8834476

15. Perez, L., Wang, J.: The effectiveness of data augmentation in image classification using deep learning. ArXiv, December 2017

16. Perez Lorenzo, C.: Detección precoz de cáncer de piel en imágenes basado en redes convolucionales. Technical report, Universidad Autónoma de Madrid (2019)

17. Pinheiro, P.: 10 Síntomas de la Anemia. Pagina Web (2020). https://www.mdsaude.com/es/hematologia-es/sintomas-de-la-anemia/

18. Redmon, J., Divvala, S., Girshick, R., Farhadi, A.: You only look once: unified, real-time object detection. IN: Proceedings of the IEEE Conference on Computer Vision and Pattern Recognition, June 2015. http://arxiv.org/abs/1506.02640

19. Reyes, J.F., Montealegre, J.S., Castano, Y.J., Urcuqui, C., Navarro, A.: LSTM and convolution networks exploration for Parkinson's diagnosis. In: 2019 IEEE Colombian Conference on Communications and Computing (COLCOM). IEEE, June 2019. https://doi.org/10.1109/ColComCon.2019.8809160

20. Rodríguez, G.P., Tuero, B.B., Acosta, S.J., Camejo, O.M.: la anemia aspectos nutricionales. conceptos actualizados para su prevención y control (2007)

21. Rojas, P.M.W., Noriega, L.A.M., Silva, A.S.: Hemoglobin screening using cloud based mobile photography applications. Ingenieria y Universidad **23**(2) (2019). https://doi.org/10.11144/javeriana.iyu23-2.hsuc

22. Saldivar-Espinoza, B., Núñez-Fernández, D., Porras-Barrientos, F., Alva-Mantari, A., Leslie, L.S., Zimic, M.: Portable system for the prediction of anemia based on the ocular conjunctiva using Artificial Intelligence. In: 33rd Conference on Neural Information Processing Systems, pp. 1–3, October 2019

23. Tang, J., Kobzarev, I., Vaughan, B.: android-demo-app. GitHub Repository (2020). https://github.com/pytorch/android-demo-app

24. Wang, C.Y., Liao, H.Y.M., Yeh, I.H., Wu, Y.H., Chen, P.Y., Hsieh, J.W.: CSPNet: a new backbone that can enhance learning capability of CNN. ArXiv, November 2019

25. Wu, Y.Y., et al.: A hematologist-level deep learning algorithm (BMSNet) for assessing the morphologies of single nuclear balls in bone marrow smears: algorithm development. JMIR Med. Inf. **8**(4), e15963 (2020). https://doi.org/10.2196/15963

On the Use of Convolutional Neural Network Architectures for Facial Emotion Recognition

Andrés Espinel⬝, Noel Pérez⬝, Daniel Riofrío⬝, Diego S. Benítez(✉)⬝, and Ricardo Flores Moyano⬝

Colegio de Ciencias e Ingenierías "El Politécnico", Universidad San Francisco de Quito USFQ, Quito 170157, Ecuador
asespinel@alumni.usfq.edu.ec,
{nperez,driofrioa,dbenitez,rflores}@usfq.edu.ec

Abstract. This work compares face gesture recognition methods based on deep learning convolutional neural network and autoencoder architectures named *DCNN1, DCNN2, DCNN3, DCNN4*, and *DCNN+Autoencoder*, that maximize the classification performance on single and mixing databases. We validated the proposed architectures on four different databases: *Jaffe, CK+, FACES*, and the combination of them over a five-fold cross-validation strategy. The *DCNN4* was the best model in the *Jaffe* and *FACES* databases, obtaining accuracy scores of 95% and 97%, respectively. The *DCNN2* achieved the best accuracy performance of 94% in the *CK+* database. Finally, the *DCNN+Autoencoder* stands as the best model in the combination of all databases (*Jaffe & CK+ & FACES*), achieving an accuracy score of 92%. Moreover, according to the cross-entropy loss function, the best model per database did not incur overfitting.

Keywords: Face emotion recognition · Face gesture classification · Deep-learning models · Artificial intelligence · Face images

1 Introduction

The recognition of human gestures is a sub-branch of computer vision that uses biometric devices such as cameras. Human gestures are captured, and then different algorithms are in charge of interpreting and recognizing emotions or movement patterns. At the present, gesture recognition has a wide field of application, such as monitoring of medical patients, control in virtual games, navigation of virtual environments, forensics research, body language interpretation, among others [9]. Regarding to neurology field, studies on facial expressions are critical for analyzing the behavior of people. In this context, Gordillo-León [10] argues that facial expressions of emotions represent an utter important mechanism to

Work funded by Universidad San Francisco de Quito (USFQ).

communicate the state of situations. Thus, facial expressions of anger or sadness might be considered responses to situations of abuse, disagreements or stress, while positive experiences provide joy expressions.

According to Sajjad *et al.* [26], facial expressions recognition (FER) systems are mainly composed of three modules: face detection, face features extraction and facial expression recognition. For instance, Ronchetti [25] propose using depth and RGB cameras to capture gestures and signs of faces, creating a database with 3200 videos and 64 different face gestures. This approach used Markovo and feed-forward back-propagation artificial neural networks models to classify facial signs based on the position and gestures of the faces.

Similarly, Pantic and Rothkrantz [22] perform a facial gestures classification whenever the subject was talking or not. Authors also carried out an experimental study on facial muscle actions typical for speech articulation. The latter was based on applying an HSV (Hue, Saturation, Value) color-based segmentation of the face. Then, identifying the zones of interest was analyzed by a trained Jordan Recurrent Neural Network (JRNN).

Nowadays, convolutional neural networks (CNN) based models have gained popularity in computer vision to face image labeling problems. In this regard, several models have adapted CNNs for facial emotion recognition (FER) alongside data augmentation and data preprocessing techniques. For example, OpenCV, a highly optimized computer vision and machine learning software library [1], includes a deep CNN for face recognition and emotion classification. In the work presented by Mayya *et al.* [21], OpenCV algorithms were used for features extraction and image classification, achieving an accuracy (ACC) of 98% when used with the *Jaffe* dataset. Similarly, Goodfellow *et al.* [8] use OpenCV to get bounding boxes around each face of the databases and then have humans doing the cropping and all the corrections necessary to feed the CNNs models for feature extraction and classification obtaining an ACC of 65% on a single dataset. A complementary approach is proposed by Li *et al.* [17] wherein OpenCV is used in conjunction with a 2-channel deep CNN for processing raw images and LBP (Local Binary Pattern) maps, achieving an ACC of 96% on a single dataset.

In the work presented by Zhang *et al.* [31], other CNNs based extensions such as WDCNN (Wide First-layer Kernels) and WMCNN-LSTM (Long short-term memory), were implemented in two different networks for training in combination with two partial VGG16 networks for classification, these models obtained an ACC of 88% on a single dataset.

Decontaminating images by using infrared (IR) spectrum is proposed by Wu *et al.* [29]. Resulting images are fed into a partial VGG DCNN and to a shallow CNN for classification, this proposal implements a confusion matrix with an overall ACC of 92% on a Caucasian dataset. While, Li and Xu [16] propose using a Discriminative Deep multi-task learning CNN (DDMTL), a k-nearestneighbor (kNN) model and an optimization module based on softmax and contrastive loss functions. This architecture provides an overall ACC of 67% and 55% on different combinations of Caucasian and Asian datasets.

Regarding to emotion classification, a deep CNN as a robust image selector together with a CNN model is proposed by Zheng *et al.* [32]. This architecture obtained an ACC of 59% when combining information of two Caucasian datasets. Moreover, a DCNN with residual blocks is implemented to reach an ACC score of 93% on a dataset of Asian faces [13].

While, a category-based support vector machine (SVM) model that uses two or more samples of different classes or expressions is presented by Farajzadeh and Hashemzadeh [7]. In order to encode the faces, this architecture computes the HOG (histogram of oriented gradients) and LBP features from each sample. In this feature space, the SVM classifier obtains a maximum ACC score of 97% on a Caucasian dataset. Finally, the combination of different micro-action-pattern modules with a deep CNN to generate more abstract mid-level semantics is presented by Liu *et al.* [18]. The architecture combines two distinct datasets, achieving ACC scores of 72.2%, 29.43%, 93.46%, and 25% on different combinations of Caucasians and Asian datasets.

Despite the evolution and development in FER, most of proposals encountered in the state of the art are focused on facial recognition on single datasets. The option of applying FER architectures on mixed datasets is partially addressed. Besides, the levels of ACC reported by these proposals are, in general, poor. In this light, a face gesture recognition method based on deep learning architectures that maximizes the classification performance on single and mixed datasets is presented in this paper.

1.1 Face Gesture Databases

We considered three public databases with samples of different ethnicities, poses, sizes, and lighting conditions, to carry out our study. A brief description of each database is next:

2 Materials and Methods

– **Jaffe:** it stands for Japanese Female Facial Expression, is a face database consisting of 213 images of 7 facial expressions (classes) posed by 10 Japanese women. These expressions are labeled by the word: happy, sad, disgust, surprise, fear, anger, and neutral. In total, there are 30 images for anger, 32 images for fear, 29 images for disgust, 31 images for happiness, 30 images for neutral, 31 images for sadness, and 30 images for surprise. All images are 256 × 256 on gray level, in TIFF (Tag Image File Format) format with no compression applied [20].
– **CK+:** it is the second version on the Cohn-Kanade database (CK). However, this database includes posed and spontaneous expressions. It was applied to 210 subjects or posers between 18 to 50 years of age from different races [14]. For the posed facial expressions, 123 subjects performed 593 sequences. A sequence is defined as the transition of a neutral expression to a peak expression. The peak expression is coded with one emotion label (same as in the

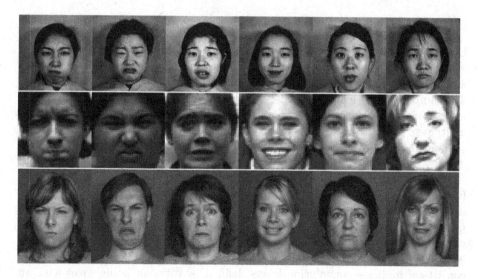

Fig. 1. An example of facial gestures, from left to right: anger, disgust, fear, happiness, neutral, and sadness from *Jaffe* [20] (top row), from *CK+* [19] (middle row), and from *FACES* (bottom row) databases.

Jaffe database). On the other hand, the spontaneous expressions are counted from 66 subjects who smiled at the camera between pose expressions. Images are either 640 × 490, or 640 × 480 pixels arrays of 8-bit gray level or 24-bit color values [19]. Out of the 593 video sequences, 327 videos were labeled with 7 emotions (classes): anger, contempt (neutral), sadness, happiness, fear, disgust, and surprise. Our experiments took static images from those video sequences to create a database of 120 images for anger, 100 images for fear, 135 images for disgust, 128 images for happiness, 94 images for contempt (neutral), 105 images for sadness, and 149 images for surprise. A total of 831 images were created.

– **FACES:** the FACES database [6] comprises a set of images of natural expression faces corresponding to 171 young (n = 58), middle-aged (n = 56), and older (n = 57) women and men displaying each six different facial expressions: neutrality, sadness, disgust, fear, anger, and happiness. The dataset was compiled at the Center for Lifespan Psychology within the Max Planck Institute for Human Development, Berlin, Germany. There are two sets of six facial expressions images (Set A and Set B) per person and expression in the FACES database; thus, it includes 2,052 individual images in total. Images have a size of 819 × 1,024 pixels resolution and are saved in JPEG format.

In this study, we considered the facial expressions that are common elements among all databases. For example, *Jaffe* and *CK+* databases contain the surprise facial expression; however, the FACES database lacks this expression. Therefore, only the interception set of facial expressions was included in the experiment, such as anger, disgust, fear, happiness, neutral, and sadness. An example of these expressions per database is shown in Fig. 1.

2.1 Deep-Learning Models

Deep learning is composed of a group of algorithms that learn from data. These algorithms are based on the structure and function of the brain's neural networks [5]. These models are trendy when dealing with classification problems. The simplest deep learning model is called a feed-forward neural network. A fully-connected architecture, also called deep feed-forward networks, aims to feed multilayer perceptrons to approximate the output of a given function like the sigmoid function [12]. However, fully-connected networks are prone to commit data over-fitting.

Deep CNNs represent one of the different deep-learning models that are used for image visualization and classification. These networks are regularized versions of a multilayered fully-connected network. Deep CNNs apply hierarchical patterns of data to assemble a more complex pattern using smaller samples, rather than the traditional approach used by a fully-connected network, that is based on the magnitude measurement of weights to the loss function [4]. It consists of multiple convolution layers defined by different kernel sizes with an activation function that connects the next layer. Pooling layers and dropout layers (to avoid overfitting) can also be found. At the end of every CNN or DCNN, there is at least one fully-connected layer with an output matching the number of classes to be classified. The main goal is to reduce the spatial variance and extract the essential features in an image for classification.

An autoencoder can be implemented alongside a DCNN architecture. The main goal is to compress data from an input layer (encoder) and then uncompress the output into a close approximation of the original input [3]. This process reduces the spatial variance and minimizes the noise in an image.

2.2 Proposed Models

In the present work, five different deep CNN models were implemented, with one of them using an autoencoder scheme. The *DCNN1*, *DCNN2*, *DCNN3*, and *DCNN4* are based on the deep CNN architecture. The *DCNN+Autoencoder* is based on the combination of a deep CNN architecture and a deep feed-forward network on an autoencoder topology. These models were empirically developed to explore their strengths in facial emotion classification.

The proposed models are inspired by the VGG16 architecture [28], which won the Imagenet competition in 2014. The VGG16 model uses kernels of 3×3 sizes and max-pooling layers with sizes 2×2 and a stride of 2 units. Then, there are two fully-connected layers with a softmax activation function. The proposed models are an extension of the VGG16 architecture, including variations of the kernel sizes in different layers to 5×5 and 3×3. Also, the number of convolution layers was reduced from 16 to 3 and 4 layers.

For a better understanding of the proposed method, we focused our description based on the *DCNN3* and *DCNN+Autoencoder* model, as shown in Fig. 2. The *DCNN3* model receives an input image with size (48×48) that transits through a convolution layer with six filters and a kernel size of 5×5 where the

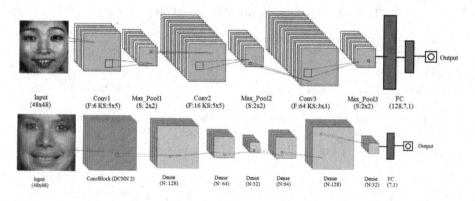

Fig. 2. Workflow of the *DCNN3* (top row) and *DCNN+Autoencoder* (bottom row) models; F - number of filters; KS - kernel size; S - max-pooling size; ConvBlock (DCNN3)

main features of the input image are extracted (see Fig. 2, top row). A max-pooling layer of size 2×2 is then applied to reduce the spatial variance in the features extracted by the first layer. The same process is applied two more times, but in this case, we used a convolution layer of 16 filters with a kernel size of 5 × 5 followed by another convolution layer of 64 filters with a kernel size of 3 × 3. Also, there is a max-pooling layer at the end of each convolution layer of the same size (2×2). Then, it flattens the output of the last convolutional layer to use it as an input of the fully-connected layer (128,7,1 neurons), which provides the final classification (output).

On the other hand, the *DCNN+Autoencoder* model first uses a convolution block, as described in the *DCNN3* model, followed by an autoencoder topology with a deep feed-forward (fully-connected) model (see Fig. 2, bottom row). In this network, after the convolution block, the flattened input image passes through an encoder process on the first three dense layers with 128, 64, and 32 neurons, respectively. After that, the decoding process starts with the information in the latent space of the network (code) and feeds three more dense layers with 64, 128, and 32 neurons, respectively. This generates a compressed version of the original data, which passes to a final fully-connected layer of (7,1) neurons for the final classification.

The remaining deep models, *DCNN1*, *DCNN2*, and *DCNN4* follow the same logic of the *DCNN3* architecture but with some variations in the convolution layers. The core architecture of all the proposed models are summarized in Table 1.

2.3   Experimental Setup

Image Preprocessing: all images were processed to keep only the area of interest inside the image (the facial area without ears and hair). Thus, we used the frontal face cascade classifier method from the OpenCV library to crop the facial area of each image. Keeping only the facial information allows us to reduce

Table 1. Core architecture of proposed deep models

DCNN1	DCNN2	DCNN3	DCNN4	DCNN+Autoencoder
Conv. (64) + Kernel (3 × 3)	Conv. (6) + Kernel (5 × 5)	Conv. (6) + Kernel (5 × 5)	Conv. (6) + Kernel (5 × 5)	Conv. (6) + Kernel (5 × 5)
Max-pooling (2 × 2)	Max-pooling (2 × 2)	Max-pooling (2 × 2)	Max-pooling (2 × 2)	Max-pooling (2 × 2)
Conv. (128) + Kernel (5 × 5)	Conv. (16) + Kernel (5× 5)	Conv. (16) + Kernel (5 × 5)	Conv. (16) + Kernel (5 × 5)	Conv. (16) + Kernel (5 × 5)
Max-pooling (2 × 2)	Max-pooling (2 × 2)	Max-pooling (2 × 2)	Max-pooling (2 × 2)	Max-pooling (2 × 2)
Conv. (512) + Kernel (3 × 3)	Conv. (64) + Kernel (5 × 5)	Conv. (64) + Kernel (3 × 3)	Conv. (120) + Kernel (3 × 3)	Conv. (64) + Kernel (3 × 3)
Max-pooling (2 × 2)	Max-pooling (2 × 2)	Max-pooling (2 × 2)	Max-pooling (2 × 2)	Max-pooling (2 × 2)
Conv. (512) + Kernel (3 × 3)	Dense (128)	Dense (128)	Dense (128)	Dense (128)
Max-pooling (2 × 2)	Fully connected (7,1)	Dense(64)	Fully connected (7,1)	Dense (64)
Dense (256)		Dense (32)		Dense (32)
Dense (512)		Dense (32)		Dense (64)
Fully connected (7,1)		Fully connected (7,1)		Dense (128)
				Dense (32)
				Fully connected (7,1)

noise and fed the classification models with relevant information. Moreover, all images were converted to grayscale level and resized to meet the required input size (48×48) of the proposed models and normalized with the min-max technique to avoid data dispersions during the model's learning. We set the input image size for both databases empirically, but a bit upper of the resize value (32×32) used in [30], which provided good classification scores.

Additionally, data augmentation techniques were implemented to increase the number of samples per class, create balanced class databases, and facilitate the learning process of the models without overfitting. Thus, operations such as rescale, shear range, zoom range, rotation range, width shift range, and height shift range were applied to achieve approximately 6867 images per database. This technique was previously used in [23,27] to face another image classification problem, obtaining successful performances.

Training and Test Partitions: for all augmented databases, the stratified 5-fold cross-validation method [11] was applied. In this way, samples are divided into disjoint training and test partitions per fold, with samples representing each output class. Training and testing the models on different partitions guarantee successful learning and further generalization.

Models Configuration: for all models, we optimized two main hyperparameters, the training iterations (epochs) in the range from 1 to 100 epochs, and the batch size was set to 32 and 64. Other parameters were used with a standard (fixed) configuration, such as the same *adam* optimizer, which uses the stochastic gradient descent to update the weights of the models during the training process [2]. The learning rate was set to $1 \cdot 10^{-2}$ and the dropouts value to 25% at the end of each convolution layer.

Assessment Metrics: we used the mean of accuracy (ACC) to validate the performance of proposed models over five folds. The cross-entropy loss function is also used to assess the probability of a given input sample being classified in the correct class. The more the loss's score is close to zero, the better classification of the input sample [15].

Selection Criteria: the best model will be selected according to the following criteria: (1) the higher mean of ACC score among all models and (2) if there is a tied performance score, the model with the least algorithm complexity is preferred.

The implementation of the proposed models was made in *Python* programming language version 3.8.3 [24] using *scikit-learn (SKlearn)*, *Keras* with *ImageDataGenerator*, and *TensorFlow* backend.

3   Results and Discussion

Each model was trained and tested on each individual dataset, and then the datasets were combined into the *Jaffe & CK+ & FACES* dataset for further experimentations. The overall values of ACC, datasets, and hyperparameters after evaluating each model are summarized in Table 2. In general, the proposed deep-learning models gave accuracy values above 85%, which is remarkable to deal with the classification problem. The main exception was the *DCNN1* model that obtained very poor results: the maximum ACC was 55% on the *CK+* dataset followed by 44% on the *FACES* dataset and 42% on the *Jaffe & CK+ & FACES* dataset. This network is the most complex which suggests that it extracts too many irrelevant features and thus decreasing the performance of the network.

For the *Jaffe* dataset, the more optimal results arrived on the *DCNN4* model. This model provided 95% ACC on the 100th epoch and a batch size of 64. The *DCNN4* architecture creates 120 kernels on the last convolution layer. This is the biggest convolution output layer of all the architectures allowing the network to extract more important features. Due to the low number of 10 subjects in the *Jaffe* dataset, the network can recognize and extract more features easily. The increased number of kernels facilitates the generalization and extraction of features in an already low variance dataset due to the low number of subjects. The *DCNN2* and *DCNN+Autoencoder* had similar results (92% and 93%), but the *DCNN3* network scored a lower ACC of 75% due to the worst feature abstraction from the complexity of this architecture.

Table 2. Performance results of deep learning Models on the three databases.

Architecture	Input shape	Optimizer	Learning rate	Batch size	Epochs	Jaffe ACC	CK+ ACC	FACES ACC	Jaffe & CK+ & FACES ACC
DCNN1	(48, 48, 1)	adam	$1 \cdot 10^{-2}$	32	25	10	15	17	12
				32	50	14	22	18	14
				32	75	17	27	21	17
				32	100	19	29	24	21
				64	25	11	45	22	17
				64	50	13	48	28	24
				64	75	14	53	36	32
				64	100	16	55	44	42
DCNN2	(48, 48, 3)	adam	$1 \cdot 10^{-2}$	32	25	76	73	70	68
				32	50	83	80	76	73
				32	75	88	83	82	76
				32	100	90	85	88	78
				64	25	78	87	78	71
				64	50	86	91	83	76
				64	75	91	93	87	78
				64	100	93	**94**	91	82
DCNN3	(48, 48, 3)	adam	$1 \cdot 10^{-2}$	32	25	43	74	68	69
				32	50	54	77	73	74
				32	75	57	79	77	76
				32	100	59	80	82	79
				64	25	50	70	75	75
				64	50	66	76	82	78
				64	75	73	80	87	82
				64	100	75	81	92	84
DCNN4	(48, 48, 3)	adam	$1 \cdot 10^{-2}$	32	25	64	69	78	70
				32	50	72	74	81	74
				32	75	77	82	84	79
				32	100	82	85	87	82
				64	25	77	70	81	66
				64	50	89	76	87	78
				64	75	93	84	94	86
				64	100	**95**	90	**97**	89
DCNN+Autoencoder	(48, 48, 3)	adam	$1 \cdot 10^{-2}$	32	25	55	64	70	60	54
				32	50	68	75	66	63
				32	75	72	77	70	66
				32	100	80	83	75	70
				64	25	50	67	77	73
				64	50	68	80	82	82
				64	75	84	83	85	86
				64	100	92	90	88	**92**

ACC - mean of the ACC metric over five folds.

For the *CK+* dataset, the better results appeared on the *DCNN2* model. In reality, this architecture achieved 94% ACC on the 100th epoch and a batch size of 64. The *DCNN2* architecture is the least complex network; it only implements three convolution layers and one fully connected layer before the output layer. The *CK+* dataset has a wide variety of subjects that grant the model the ability to generalize features without needing too many convolutional layers. The *DCNN4* model and the *DCNN+Autoencoder* had the same ACC. On the other hand, the *DCNN3* architecture obtained the worst ACC of 81% from the difficulty of extracting relevant features of this model.

For the *FACES* dataset, the *DCNN4* model achieved the better results. This approach achieved an outstanding score of 97% on the 100th and a batch size of 64. The last convolution layer helps the model to better extract features from all the subjects on the dataset. In addition, the last dense layer of 128 neurons allows the architecture to filter not relevant features and reach better clasifications. The *DCNN2* and the *DCNN3* models had similar results (91% and 92%) and the *DCNN+Autoencoder* had the worst results overall with 88% ACC.

Finally, for the combination of the *Jaffe* & *CK+* & *FACES* dataset, the approach *DCNN+Autoencoder* reached better results. This model scored 92% ACC on the 100th epoch and a batch size of 64. When combining both datasets, it is more difficult to extract relevant features due to the noise generated by this combination. The autoencoder architecture helps to reduce the noise and the spatial variance of each image. In this context, an autoencoder topology will outperform the rest of the models. The rest of architectures (*DCNN2*, *DCNN3* and *DCNN4*) achieved around 85% ACC on this dataset.

According to our selection criteria, the *DCNN+Autoencoder* architecture outperformed the rest of the models due to the highest ACC obtained. Moreover, this network also achieved high accuracies in the datasets individually: 92% on the Jaffe dataset 90% on the CK+ dataset and 88% on the FACES dataset. Besides, the best architectures for each dataset experimentation dealt with the overfitting problem effectively. Following the plots presented in Fig. 3 the curves of the mean validation loss are very similar to the curves of the mean training loss for the *Jaffe*, *CK+*, *FACES* and *Jaffe* & *CK+* & *FACES*. The plot for the *Jaffe* dataset indicates the training loss and the validation loss start converging

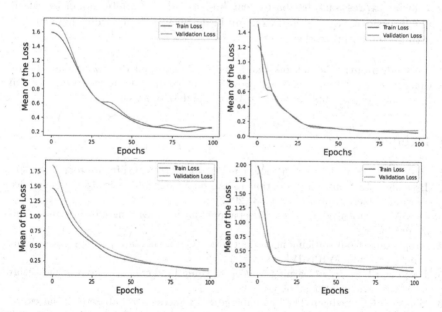

Fig. 3. Performance of the mean cross-entropy loss function over five folds for the best model on the *Jaffe* (top left), *CK+* (top right), *FACES* (bottom left) and *Jaffe* & *CK+* & *FACES* (bottom right) databases.

at the 10th epoch on the *DCNN4* model; the same scenario reproduces for the *Jaffe* & *CK+* & *FACES* dataset on the *DCNN+Autoencoder* architecture. In addition, the curves start converging on 70th epoch or the *FACES* dataset on the *DCNN4* model. Lastly, the curves start converging on the 75th epoch for the *CK+* dataset on the *DCNN2* network. This shows that our architectures are good for generalization on the testing sets distinct from the training sets.

4   Conclusions and Future Work

In this work, five different deep CNN and autoencoder architectures were validated on four different databases, the *Jaffe*, *CK+*, *FACES*, and a combination of them using a stratified five-fold cross-validation method. The obtained results highlighted the *DCNN4* model as the best method for the *Jaffe* and *FACES* databases, achieving 95% and 97% ACC scores, respectively. The *DCNN2* model was the best for the *CK+* database, obtaining an ACC score of 94%, and the *DCCN+Autoencoder* model was the winner when combined all databases as a unique dataset, reaching an ACC score of 92%. The *DCNN1* model had the worst results overall due to high loss values and big overfitting problems, and shallow accuracy values in all datasets (19%, 55%, 44%, and 42%). Except for the *DCNN1*, the remaining models avoided being stuck in overfitting as reported by the cross-entropy loss function.

As future work, we plan to explore further other deep learning models and more facial expressions databases searching for the ultimate model to classify facial expressions. Also, to carry out an in-depth search of models hyperparameters to better optimize them.

Acknowledgment. The authors thank the Applied Signal Processing and Machine Learning Research Group USFQ for providing the computing infrastructure (NVidia DGX workstation) to implement and execute the developed source code.

References

1. Bradski, G., Kaehler, A.: Opencv. Dr. Dobb's journal of software tools **3** (2000)
2. Brownlee, J.: Gentle introduction to the adam optimization algorithm for deep learning. Mach. Learn. Mastery **3** (2017)
3. DeepAI: Autoencoder. https://deepai.org/machine-learning-glossary-and-terms/autoencoder
4. DeepLizard: Convolutional neural networks (CNNs) explained. https://deeplizard.com/learn/video/YRhxdVk_sIs
5. DeepLizard: Machine learning & deep learning fundamentals. https://deeplizard.com/learn/video/OT1jslLoCyA
6. Ebner, N.C., Riediger, M., Lindenberger, U.: Faces—a database of facial expressions in young, middle-aged, and older women and men: development and validation. Behav. Res. Methods **42**(1), 351–362 (2010)
7. Farajzadeh, N., Hashemzadeh, M.: Exemplar-based facial expression recognition. Inf. Sci. **460**, 318–330 (2018)

8. Goodfellow, I.J., et al.: Challenges in representation learning: a report on three machine learning contests. In: Lee, M., Hirose, A., Hou, Z.-G., Kil, R.M. (eds.) ICONIP 2013. LNCS, vol. 8228, pp. 117–124. Springer, Heidelberg (2013). https://doi.org/10.1007/978-3-642-42051-1_16

9. Gordillo, F., Arana, J.M., Meilán, J.J.G., Mestas, L., Pérez, M.Á.: The timely expression of coherence helps cause the right impression. Anales de Psicología/Ann. Psychol. **33**(2), 211–217 (2017)

10. Gordillo-León, D.F.: Effect of Verbal context and facial expression on impression formation - Efecto del contexto verbal y la expresión facial sobre la formación de impresiones. Ph.D. thesis, Universidad de Salamanca (2018)

11. Gupta, P.: Cross validation in machine learning. https://towardsdatascience.com/cross-validation-in-machine-learning-72924a69872f

12. Gupta, P.: Deep learning: Feedforward neural network. https://towardsdatascience.com/deep-learning-feedforward-neural-network-26a6705dbdc7

13. Jain, D.K., Shamsolmoali, P., Sehdev, P.: Extended deep neural network for facial emotion recognition. Pattern Recognit. Lett. **120**, 69–74 (2019)

14. Kanade, T., Cohn, J.F., Tian, Y.: Comprehensive database for facial expression analysis. In: Proceedings Fourth IEEE International Conference on Automatic Face and Gesture Recognition (Cat. No. PR00580), pp. 46–53 (2000). https://doi.org/10.1109/AFGR.2000.840611

15. Koech, K.E.: Cross-entropy loss function. https://towardsdatascience.com/cross-entropy-loss-function-f38c4ec8643e

16. Li, H., Xu, H.: Deep reinforcement learning for robust emotional classification in facial expression recognition. Knowl. Based Syst. **204**, 106172 (2020)

17. Li, J., Jin, K., Zhou, D., Kubota, N., Ju, Z.: Attention mechanism-based CNN for facial expression recognition. Neurocomputing **411**, 340–350 (2020)

18. Liu, M., Li, S., Shan, S., Chen, X.: Au-inspired deep networks for facial expression feature learning. Neurocomputing **159**, 126–136 (2015)

19. Lucey, P., Cohn, J.F., Kanade, T., Saragih, J., Ambadar, Z., Matthews, I.: The extended Cohn-Kanade dataset (CK+): a complete dataset for action unit and emotion-specified expression. In: 2010 IEEE Computer Society Conference on Computer Vision and Pattern Recognition-Workshops, pp. 94–101. IEEE (2010)

20. Lyons, M., Kamachi, M., Gyoba, J.: The Japanese Female Facial Expression (JAFFE) Dataset, April 1998. https://doi.org/10.5281/zenodo.3451524

21. Mayya, V., Pai, R.M., Pai, M.M.: Automatic facial expression recognition using DCNN. Procedia Comput. Sci. **93**, 453–461 (2016)

22. Pantic, M., Rothkrantz, L.: Facial gesture recognition in face image sequences: a study on facial gestures typical for speech articulation, vol. 6, p. 6, November 2002. https://doi.org/10.1109/ICSMC.2002.1175613

23. Peña, A., Pérez, N., Benítez, D.S., Hearn, A.: Tracking hammerhead sharks with deep learning. In: 2020 IEEE Colombian Conference on Applications of Computational Intelligence (IEEE ColCACI 2020), pp. 1–6. IEEE (2020). https://doi.org/10.1109/ColCACI50549.2020.9247911

24. Python Core Team: Python 3.6.9: A dynamic, open source programming language. Python Software Foundation (2019), https://www.python.org/

25. Ronchetti, F.: Recognition of dynamic gestures and its application to sign language - Reconocimiento de gestos dinámicos y su aplicación al lenguaje de señas. In: XX Workshop de Investigadores en Ciencias de la Computacion (WICC 2018), Universidad Nacional del Nordeste (2018)

26. Sajjad, M., Nasir, M., Ullah, F.U.M., Muhammad, K., Sangaiah, A.K., Baik, S.W.: Raspberry Pi assisted facial expression recognition framework for smart security in law-enforcement services. Inf. Sci. **479**, 416–431 (2019)
27. Salazar, A., Arroyo, R., Pérez, N., Benítez, D.: Deep-learning for volcanic seismic events classification. In: 2020 IEEE Colombian Conference on Applications of Computational Intelligence (IEEE ColCACI 2020), pp. 1–6. IEEE (2020). https://doi.org/10.1109/ColCACI50549.2020.9247848
28. Simonyan, K., Zisserman, A.: Very deep convolutional networks for large-scale image recognition. arXiv preprint arXiv:1409.1556 (2014)
29. Wu, H., Liu, Y., Liu, Y., Liu, S.: Efficient facial expression recognition via convolution neural network and infrared imaging technology. Infrared Phys. Technol. **102**, 103031 (2019)
30. Yaddaden, Y., Adda, M., Bouzouane, A., Gaboury, S., Bouchard, B.: User action and facial expression recognition for error detection system in an ambient assisted environment. Expert Syst. Appl. **112**, 173–189 (2018). https://doi.org/10.1016/j.eswa.2018.06.033
31. Zhang, H., Huang, B., Tian, G.: Facial expression recognition based on deep convolution long short-term memory networks of double-channel weighted mixture. Pattern Recognit. Lett. **131**, 128–134 (2020)
32. Zheng, H., Wang, R., Ji, W., Zong, M., Wong, W.K., Lai, Z., Lv, H.: Discriminative deep multi-task learning for facial expression recognition. Inf. Sci. **533**, 60–71 (2020)

Automated Preprocessing Pipeline in Visual Imagery Tasks

Christian Camilo Rosero-Rodríguez and Wilfredo Alfonso-Morales[✉]

School of Electrical and Electronics Engineering
Universidad del Valle, Santiago de Cali, Colombia
{christian.camilo.rosero,wilfredo.alfonso}@correounivalle.edu.co

Abstract. The EEG recordings contain complex and high-resolution temporal information, representing great challenges from the point of view of data processing: high contamination of artifacts, large sample sizes, reproducibility of the procedure, and the number of EEG channels. However, traditional approaches still use manual rejection, which is unsustainable. This article proposes an automatic preprocessing procedure for shared neural representations between imagery and visual perception over four frequency bands (theta, alpha, low beta, high beta). The idea is to improve the feature extraction procedure by identifying and interpolating faulty channels and rejecting bad epochs due to significantly noisy signals. Here, we include multiple filtering steps, robust common reference with PREP, artifact rejection, noisily channel identification and interpolation, and faulty epoch reconstruction and rejection to improve multivariate pattern analysis - MVPA. This latter represents the data decoding accuracy on the time-frequency domain.

Keywords: Visual imagery · Visual perception · Preprocessing · Brain-computer interfaces

1 Introduction

The numerous advances in the development and implementation of BCIs are driven by scientific and technological achievements, as well as social and commercial demands [4]. Among the potential applications of BCIs is the recognition of mental imagery, which is the representation of sensory information, in the absence of a direct external stimulus when it is retrieved from memory or previous perceptual input [9,20]. A special type of mental image is the visual image whose neural representation of the associated entity, initially introduced exogenously, is reactivated endogenously from long-term memory and is kept in visuospatial working memory to be inspected and transformed [9,23].

The exogenous paradigms of BCI, such as the P300 and SSVEP, have several drawbacks [18], since they already require external stimuli and additional visualization equipment. In addition, the mental tasks used in these paradigms can be

A. D. Orjuela-Cañón et al. (Eds.): ColCACI 2021, CCIS 1471, pp. 31–52, 2022.
https://doi.org/10.1007/978-3-030-91308-3_3

complex and not very intuitive to carry out as they have little or no correlation with the message to be communicated with the BCI [18].

The use of visual mental images is a mechanism for communicating intentions or ideas, which turns out to be the most natural and intuitive [4,18], since the flow of information from detailed images in the brain is faster and most of its sensory experience is visual, with the ability to experience different colors, shapes and textures [8], allowing the user's intention to be directly decoded [18]. Studies show that neural representations of visual perceptual and mental images resemble each other, sharing common mechanisms in the occipital (visual), parietal, and frontal cortex [2,7,8,10,16,20,23].

The recognition of mental images is a perception challenge that requires sufficiently robust extraction and classification algorithms that show the neural representation of the endogenous form from the memory of each user. Different algorithms and computational intelligence techniques are increasingly used in neuroscience to classify brain signals for BCI [1,17] due to the challenges generated by the intrinsic nature of EEG signals. Some challenges as the low signal-to-noise ratio, their non-stationarity in time, the variance of the signals within the intra-user tests, the limited amount of data to train the classifiers, and the low general confidence (validity) of the current BCI systems [17].

The research efforts have focused on identifying and designing solutions that address the classification problem-oriented to EEG-based BCIs [17], such that the results provide a precision that exceeds the levels of theoretical probability and are statistically significant [5]. Furthermore, during the acquisition of the EEG signal, it suffers from contamination, both external and internal to the participant [12]. This contamination can be so strong that in many cases, these artifacts are much more prominent than the neurophysiological signal, so if left uncorrected, they can significantly distort the EEG signal [12].

The classification algorithms are sensitive to preprocessing, so the lack of attention in this first stage is critical. Proper preprocessing increases the signal-to-noise ratio and reduces unwanted artifacts in the data [3]. Although a series of preprocessing transformations are typically applied to the EEG signal by including filtering, artifact removal, and signal re-referencing, that process is poorly standardized or automated, making the channels and parameters for the processing of EEGs vary between different studies [3,12].

The intensive selection or editing of uncontaminated EEG data manually and expertly by the investigator is often a common artifact removal approach [12]. For example, a study on the temporal dynamics of shared representations between visual perception and imagination in [23] uses partially subjective owner criteria. That turns out to be inconsistent between individuals and with difficulties due to human error and discrepancies in judgment [12,19]. In addition, the increasing trend to perform large-scale tests of generalizability between subjects and paradigms [3], increase sample sizes, ensure reproducibility of analyzes, as well as EEG channel densities [19], make traditional processing approaches such as manual rejection unsustainable [12].

These problems are observed when analyzing and trying to replicate the study carried out in [23], whose preprocessing stage includes a visual inspection and manual removal of SSP (*Signal Space Projection*) components that resembled space properties -temporal blinks and eye movements. The selection and elimination of these components was based on subjective criteria of the researchers, which hinders the reproducibility of the study, which, although the publication of preprocessed data compensates it, presents a problem if one wants to work with raw data. Therefore, it is considered appropriate to develop an automatic preprocessing *pipeline* that improves the results obtained in [23], understanding as *pipeline* the process made up of modules or chain stages, where the input is the raw data and the output the preprocessed data. This *pipeline* seeks to be a standard component for the data of the different subjects in the study, which would provide several advantages such as the uniform application of the criteria of artifact elimination, canal repair, rejection of epochs, and flow of efficiency for large data sets. In addition, it helps to compare between them and will remove the manual inspection aspects that mainly affect the content of the signals and their relevant features.

2   Materials and Methods

The *pipeline* runs on top of MNE-Python, an open-source software package that provides state-of-the-art neuro signal algorithms implemented on top of Python [13].

Dataset. The data set, taken from the study by Xie et al. [23], demonstrates that shared representations between imagery and perception arise specifically in the *alpha* frequency band. The dataset is comprised of EEG recordings from 38 healthy participants, 30 female and 8 male, with normal or corrected visual acuity, with a mean age of 24.1 ± 4.99 years and is available from an open-access repository.[1]

The stimuli for the perception task consisted of a set of images of everyday objects (apple, carrot, rose, butterfly, chicken, sheep, car, chair, violin, ear, eye, and hand) with 12 color photographs on a gray background. For the imagination task, audio recordings of a human voice pronouncing the 12 German words corresponding to each picture were used.

A 64 channel EASYCAP system and a *Brainvision actiCHamp* amplifier were used for recording EEG data. The 64 electrodes were arranged according to the standard $10 - 10$ system, using Fz as the reference electrode. The acquisition was continuous with a sampling rate of 1 KHz, with in-line filtering between 0.3 and 100 Hz.

---

[1] https://osf.io/ykp9w/data with and without preprocessing.

Data Reading. The data is in the file format *BrainVision*, which consists of three separate files:

1. A text header file (.vhdr) containing meta-data.
2. A text marker file (.vmrk) containing information about events in the data.
3. A binary data file (.eeg) containing the voltage values of the EEG.

MNE-Python has read functions for a wide variety of EEG hardware vendor file formats, including that of *BrainVision*, using the header .vhdr file as input to the *mne.io.read_raw_brainvision()* function.[2] These results in a raw data object (*Raw*) in Neuromag's FIF format, which is the default storage format, providing a consistent interface to the meta-data of the recordings using the so-called *measurement information*. This object contains the EEG signals and displays information about the file: times, events, channel locations, applied filters, projectors, among others.

Methodology of Evaluation. The data provided by the original study will be compared with those obtained in this study following the classification and cross-validation methodology presented by Xie et al. [23], which is described below.

Quantification of Signal-to-Noise Ratio. The signal-to-noise ratio (SNR) measurement is the gold standard for quantifying signal performance after preprocessing [22], considered as a measure of the fidelity of neuro signal transmission and detection. SNR is defined as the dimensionless ratio of the power spectral density (PSD) of a signal (meaningful information) to the power of the background noise [22]. The signal-to-noise ratio that corresponds to each frequency is:

$$SNR(f) = \frac{P_S(f)}{P_N(f)} \tag{1}$$

To calculate the noise power, we use the methodology used in [6,11], where it is quantified as the difference in power in each band between the average of the individual trials (i.e., the total signal of the trials) and the magnitude of the signals averaged over all trials. That is, the noise power is the electrical power difference in each EEG band (theta, alpha, low beta, high beta) from the averaged signal, which is related to the mental task, which is composed of the background EEG activity, unrelated to task processing, and the task-related signal.

Noise power assessment may distinguish between task-related oscillations and oscillations underlying functions other than those related to the task being performed, i.e., functions likely to be active in the resting state that persists during the performance of a given task.

---

[2] Warning: To organize EEG data in BIDS format, it is often necessary to rename the files, however, renaming the *BrainVision* files can be problematic due to their multi-file structure.

Time-Frequency Decomposition. EEG data recorded for the visual perception and visual imagination tasks are convolved using the Wavelet Morlet complex, of constant length 600 ms and logarithmically spaced in 20 frequency bins between 5 Hz and 31 Hz, separately for each trial and each channel.

Thus, absolute power values are extracted for each time point and frequency via the square root of the resulting time-frequency coefficients. These values are brought to the decibel (dB) scale to reflect relative changes from the pre-stimulus baseline (-500 ms to -300 ms relative to stimulus onset). In order to increase the signal-to-noise ratio of all subsequent analyses, the time-frequency representations were reduced by averaging the data in 20 *ms* bins to obtain a temporal resolution of 50 Hz.

The 20 frequency bins were then aggregated into 4 discrete frequency bands, which were analyzed separately: theta (5–7 Hz), alpha (8–13 Hz), low beta (14–20 Hz) and high beta (21–31 Hz).

Classification of Oscillatory Responses. In order to determine the temporal dynamics of shared neural representations between perception and imagery, a Multi-Variate Pattern Analysis (MVPA) cross–validation scheme was implemented using Time-Frequency data. The latter consisted of training classifiers to discriminate pairs of objects from EEG data recorded during one task and test them on EEG data for the same two objects in the other task.

This cross-validation of perception *vs* imagery is performed using a temporal generalization variant of MVPA, which consists of creating four pseudo-trials for each condition by averaging the pattern vectors in the same condition with 25% of the available trials. It was made by the support vector machines (C-SVM with a linear kernel and a cost parameter of $c = 1$) with all possible combinations of time points for both tasks. Classification is repeated across both train-test directions, i.e., train on perception and test on imagery data, and vice versa. This process is repeated for all pairwise object combinations by calculating the classification accuracy as the average across repetitions. Finally, the entire classification analysis was repeated 100 times, with new random assignments of trials on pseudo-trials, and the results averaged over these 100 repetitions. The process in greater detail is described in [23].

2.1 Automated Preprocessing Pipeline

The pipeline consists of two parts: A part of Noise and Artifact Removal in the raw data (Continuous); and another part of Epoch Definition, where a preprocessing is also performed at the epoch level. The general diagram can be seen in Fig. 1.

Noise and Artifact Removal. This phase seeks to eliminate or attenuate noise and artifacts from exogenous (environmental) and endogenous (biological) sources in the data. For this purpose, the preprocessing performed in [23] is taken into account but seeking a standardized and fully automated process for all sessions

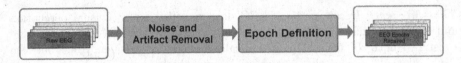

Fig. 1. Block diagram of the pipeline.

and subjects, avoiding preconceptions, prejudices, and subjective biases of the investigator.

This phase starts with a resampling, after which the preprocessing pipeline *PREP* of [3] is used to perform an initial cleaning to determine a solid reference signal and interpolate the defective channels. That is followed by detecting and removing ocular artifacts with SSP and then finished with a new re-reference. Figure 2 summarizes this phase.

Stage I: Resampling: At this stage, the raw data must be resampled to facilitate the use of computational resources. A resampling frequency of 250 Hz is chosen, taking into account that the new minimum allowable sampling frequency should not be lower than twice the maximum frequency of the low pass filter implemented in line, in this case, 100 Hz to avoid aliasing following the concept of Nyquist's Theorem.

Stage II: *pipeline* PREP: The first module after resampling is the PREP [3] pipeline. PREP offers standardized upstream preprocessing, including line denoising using the *cleanline* method and common average reference (CAR) with detection and interpolation of defective channels with respect to the reference.

Under European standards, a line frequency of 50 Hz and its harmonics was specified as the first step in PREP. To mitigate the interaction between the reference and the faulty channels, PERP's robust reference algorithm is used to prevent noisy/defective channels from irrecoverably contaminating the signal when preprocessing applies CAR prior to the detection of a faulty channel [3]. Only after the data has been re-referenced can the faulty channels [3] be calculated. In summary, the algorithm estimates the mean of the real signal and uses the re-referenced signal by this means to find the "real" faulty channels and interpolates.

PREP detects noisy channels using four criteria [3]:

1. Deviation criterion (Extreme amplitudes)
2. Correlation criterion (Low correlation between channels)
3. Predictability criterion (Low predictability)
4. Noise criterion (Unusual high-frequency noise)

Once detected, PREP performs a spherical interpolation of these channels using the EEGLAB's *eeg_interp* function, which uses *Legendre* polynomials of up to 7° [3]. At the end of this stage, we obtain continuous data re-referenced on a robust reference.

Stage III: Eye artifact repair with SSP: This stage seeks to repair or remove artifacts that may be contaminating the brain activity signals of interest.

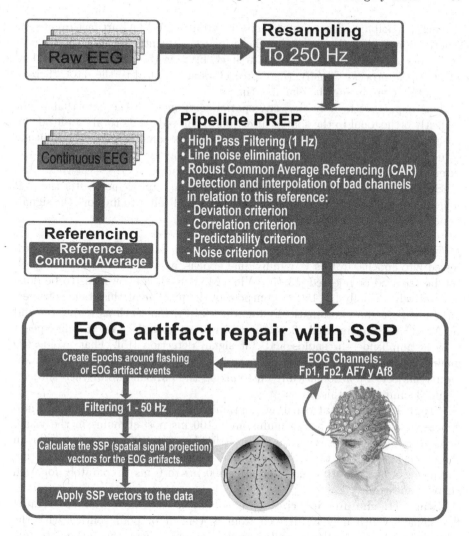

Fig. 2. Continuous data preprocessing block diagram.

One of the most common artifacts is those produced by eyeblinks and eye movements. For this purpose, we proceed by using signal space projection (SSP) [13], which projects the signal into a lower-dimensional subspace, seeking to eliminate noise from EEG signals. The subspace is chosen by calculating the average pattern between sensors when noise is present, treating that pattern as a "direction" in sensor space, and constructing the subspace to be orthogonal to the noise direction [13].

Due to the absence of EOG sensors, the frontal electrodes $Fp1$, $Fp2$, $AF7$, and $AF8$ are used to calculate the SSP projectors close to the eye muscles. According to [23] the number of calculated projectors is between one and four for each participant. First, suitable epochs around the EOG artifact events are generated by finding the electrode's flicker peaks, as mentioned above. Then SSP projectors are calculated for the eye artifact, filtering the EEG signal from 1 to 50 Hz in the process. Finally, these projectors are applied to the data, thereby eliminating or reducing the ocular artifacts.

It is important to note that any spatial component in the data that is not perfectly orthogonal to the spatial direction(s) will reduce its total amplitude by the projection operation. SSP generally introduces some amount of amplitude reduction bias into the sensor space data, so it may be useful to visualize the extent to which the SSP projection has biased them.

Stage IV: Re-referencing: Since there was an improvement after the SSP stage, a new re-referencing is performed using a CAR filter to improve the signal-to-noise ratio of the EEG signals.

Definition of Epochs. In this phase, the continuous data is segmented and processed into epochs. In this way individual epochs, as well as incorrect channels, can be repaired or rejected [13,15]. While MNE-Python allows this to be done interactively/visually [13,15], the purpose of the *pipeline* at this stage is to perform this procedure automatically for which algorithms such as *autoreject* and *RANSAC* are implemented. [3,14,15], which learn from the data to define peak-to-peak amplitude thresholds and flat signal detection [15]. That avoids the manual definition of these parameters and achieves standardization across individual subjects by automatically customizing the parameters for each subject. Figure 3 summarizes this phase.

Stage I: Segmentation: Raw continuous EEG data were segmented into epochs between 600 ms pre-stimulus and 1100 ms post-stimulus in the visual perception task and between 600 ms pre-stimulus and 3100 ms post-stimulus in the visual imagination task. Epoch data were baseline corrected by subtracting the mean of the pre-stimulus interval (−600 ms to 0 ms), separately for each channel and trial.

Stage II: channel interpolation: Channels that have produced erratic, flat signals, which may be derived from movement or poor contact with the electrode scalp during the recording session, among others, should be detected. At this stage, the *RANSAC* algorithm of the *autoreject* version of the *pipeline* PREP Bigdely-Shamlo2015 originally implemented as part of the *pipeline* PREP Bigdely-Shamlo2015 is used. In this approach, adopted for the EEG artifact detection use case, by default, the 25% channels(*inliers*) are randomly sampled, and the data in all channels are interpolated from these *inliers* channels. That is repeated several times to produce a set of 50 time series for each sensor, calculating in each, instant by instant, the correlation between the median and the actual data [3,14]. An outlier or defective channel is considered if its correlation is less than a threshold (0.75 in the PREP implementation) [3,14].

A channel that is faulty with more than 40% of the tests is flagged as globally bad and interpolated [14]; however, we do not directly use *RANSAC* is internal interpolation, which is based on the spherical *spline* algorithm, which is used to estimate the scalp potential [21], but instead use the same MNE-Python function that implements the same algorithm for modularity effects.

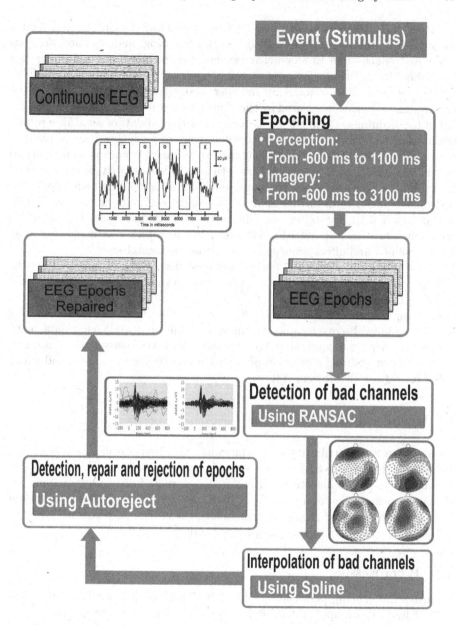

Fig. 3. Block diagram of segmented data preprocessing.

One thing to keep in mind is that although channels detected as defective could be eliminated, this would leave the data with different dimensions, which would be a problem for subsequent cross-validation analyses.

Stage III: Rejection of epochs: Once the interpolation of the defective channels is done, we continue with detecting, repairing, and rejecting the contaminated epochs due to channel noise. For this purpose, the *autoreject* [14] algorithm, from the library of the same name and compatible with MNE-Python, is used. *Autoreject* is an unsupervised algorithm that minimizes the cross-validation error, measured by the *Frobenius* norm between the average signal of the training set and the median signal of the validation set [15], a robust evaluation metric for estimating the optimal peak-to-peak threshold, a quantity commonly used to identify bad EEG epochs [14]. This approach is then extended to a more sophisticated algorithm that estimates this threshold for each channel that produces bad test/epoch channels, and the test is repaired by interpolation or by excluding it from further analysis depending on the number of bad channels detected [14]. *Autoreject* not only repairs and removes epochs containing transient jumps in isolated EEG channels, but also flicker artifacts that may have remained and affect groups of channels in the frontal area [15].

The *Autoreject* algorithm has advantages that make it suitable for the *pipeline*; it provides an automatic data-driven algorithmic solution to a task, avoiding manual analysis, reducing the cost of data inspection by experts, and eliminating their biases, thus facilitating the reproduction of results and limiting the risk of false discoveries and conclusions. Additionally, allowing data to be repaired rather than eliminated from the analysis saves costly data to acquire. It does this by defining a clear set of inclusion criteria for EEG data, and which are standard for all subjects [14].

3   Results and Discussion

To illustrate the contribution of the pipeline, data from 8 subjects (01, 02, 03, 10, 11, 15, 20, 26, 29, 34, 38) of the study were worked on. The statistics of channels detected as defective and repaired, before and after preprocessing are shown for each session and task. Also, the signal-to-noise ratio before and after preprocessing for each session and task; finally, the visual analysis of the averaged MVPA of the subjects in the 4 frequency bands was analyzed.

3.1   Preprocessing

Robust re-referencing performed by the PREP module and artifact repair performed by SSP are applied to the data for each session and task. The metrics that can be analyzed are the number, identification, and Classification of faulty channels performed by PREP on the raw data and *RANSAC* on the segmented data. That was done for each task within each session. Tables 1 and 2 show the noisy channels detected by PREP before robust re-referencing, the noisy channels detected and interpolated by PREP after robust re-referencing and the remaining noisy channels after the interpolation; furthermore, the channels detected and interpolated by *RANSAC* and Spline respectively after the PREP stage are presented.

Table 1. Table of the detected and interpolated bad electrodes for session 1 for the subjects.

Subject	Stage	Perception Channels	Amt	Imagery Channels	Amt
01	Noisy channels original		0	F7	1
	Interpolated channels	TP9	1	TP9	1
	Still noisy channels		0		0
	RANSAC	Fp1, Fp2	2	Fp1, Fp2	2
02	Noisy channels original	F2, AFz, Pz, FT10, CP3, C3, FC6	7	F2, AFz, FC6, AF3, FT10, C3, Pz	7
	Interpolated channels	FT9, FC6, T8, FT10, CP3, C3, Pz	7	FT9, FC6, T8, AF8, Fp1, FT10, C3, AF7, Pz	9
	Still noisy channels	Fp1	1	Fp2	1
	RANSAC	Fp1, O2, Fp2, AF7, AFz, P1, AF8	7	Fp1, AFz, AF4, AF8	4
03	Noisy channels original		0		0
	Interpolated channels	T8	1		0
	Still noisy channels		0		0
	RANSAC	Fp1, P8, TP10, Fp2, AF3, AFz, CP3, PO3, AF4, AF8	10	Fp1, P8, TP10, CP3, AF8	5
10	Noisy channels original	FC2, FCz, F2, AF8	4	F2, Fp2, AF4, AF8, Fp1	5
	Interpolated channels	FT10, AF8	2	Fp2, AF8, Fp1, FT10, AF7, PO4	6
	Still noisy channels	PO4	1		0
	RANSAC	Fp1, FT9, T7, Fp2, AF7, AF3, AFz, C5, P6, CPz, AF4	11	F3, FC5, Fp2, AF3, F1, F5, FC3, CPz, AF4	9
11	Noisy channels original	FC4, F2, CP4, C3, AF7	5	FC2, Cz, Fp1	3
	Interpolated channels	C6, FC4, F2, CP4, TP10, FT8, C3, AF7	8	C6, FC2, Cz, CP4, FT8, Fp1, AF7	7
	Still noisy channels		0		0
	RANSAC	F7, AFz, AF4	3	Fp2	1
15	Noisy channels original	F2	1	F2, Fp2, F1	3
	Interpolated channels	TP10, TP9	2	TP9	1
	Still noisy channels		0		0
	RANSAC	Fp1	1	Fp1	1
20	Noisy channels original	Fp2, F6, F2, AF8, AF3, F4, AF7, F3, F5, F1, AF4, FC6, FT7	13	CP1, Fp2, F2, AF3, F4, F3, AF7, Fp1, F7, F5, F1, AF4, FC6, F6	14
	Interpolated channels	Fp2, FC5, T7, AF8, AF3, AF7, TP10, F5, AF4, FC6, FT9, TP9, FT7	13	CP1, Fp2, T7, AF3, AF7, Fp1, TP10, F5, AF4, FC6, FT9, TP9, FT7	13
	Still noisy channels		0		0
	RANSAC	T8, AFz, F6	3	Fp2, AF8	2
26	Noisy channels original	F7, F4, F3	3	P4, TP9	2
	Interpolated channels	TP10, T7	2	TP10, P4, TP9	3
	Still noisy channels		0		0
	RANSAC	T8, AF7	2	Cz, CPz	2
29	Noisy channels original	Fp2, F2, CP2, F4, AF7, C2, Fp1, F7, P4, F5, F1, AF4, F6	13	Fp2, CP2, F4, AF7, C2, Fp1, P4, F6	8
	Interpolated channels	Fp2, CP2, F4, AF7, C2, F7, P4, F6	8	Fp2, CP2, AF7, C2, Fp1, F7, P4, F6	8
	Still noisy channels		0		0
	RANSAC	Fp1, Pz, F5	3	F4, F5, AF4	3
34	Noisy channels original	F2, Fp1, P4, CP4, C6, TP8, TP9	7	F2, Fp1, P4, Cz, TP8	5
	Interpolated channels	T8, CP2, FT10, Fp1, P4, Cz, C6, P6, TP8, CP4, TP9	11	T8, CP2, FT10, Fp1, P4, Cz, C6, TP8, TP9	9
	Still noisy channels		0		0
	RANSAC	T7, F8, C5, TP7, AF8	5	Fp2, F1, TP7	3
38	Noisy channels original	Fp2, F2, FCz, Fp1, F1	5	Fp2, AF8, Fp1, F5, F1	5
	Interpolated channels	T7, FCz, TP10, Fp1, FT9, FT7	6	Fp2, AF8, FT8, AF7, TP10, Fp1, FT7	7
	Still noisy channels		0		0
	RANSAC	T8, Fp2, AF3, F5, TP8, AF8	6	F7, AF3, AFz, F5, F6	5

Table 2. Table of the detected and interpolated bad electrodes for session 2 for the subjects.

Subject	Stage	Perception Channels	Amt	Imagery Channels	Amt
01	Noisy channels original	F2, F8, F4, Fp1	4	F2, AFz, AF4, F4, Fp1	5
	Interpolated channels	F2, FT7, Fp1, P6, FT10	5	F2, Fp2, FT7, Fp1, P6	5
	Still noisy channels	FT10	1		0
	RANSAC	Fp2, F5, AF4, AF8	4	F8, AF7, C2, AF8	4
02	Noisy channels original	P2, C2, F1, Pz	4	AF3, F1, Fp1	3
	Interpolated channels	FT9, C2, FT7, P2, Pz	5	FT9, T7, FT7, AF8, Fp1, FT10, AF7	7
	Still noisy channels	Fp1	1		0
	RANSAC	T8, FC6, AF7, TP7, C6, AF8	6	CP1, T8, AFz, C5, C6, AF4	6
03	Noisy channels original	F3, F1, AF3	3	F3, F1	2
	Interpolated channels	F3, AF3, T8, TP10, TP8, FC5, TP9, TP7	8	TP10, TP7	2
	Still noisy channels	C5	1		0
	RANSAC	Fp1, F7, AF7, C5, AF8	5	Fp1, AF8	2
10	Noisy channels original	F3, F2, F6, F8, AF3, AF4, F4, F5, F1	9	F3, F2, F6, F8, AF3, Fp2, AF4, F4, AF8, Fp1, F5, F1, AF7	13
	Interpolated channels	CP2, F3, F6, AF3, T7, C5, AF8, F5, TP9, AF7	10	F3, F6, AF3, T7, Fp2, F4, FT8, AF8, Fp1, F5, TP9, AF7	12
	Still noisy channels	F4	1		0
	RANSAC	Fp1, T8, Fp2	3	F8	1
11	Noisy channels original	F7, Fp2, F4, P7, F5, FT10, TP8	7	P8, F7, T8, Fp2, Fp1, F5, FT10	7
	Interpolated channels	C6, T8, TP10, P7, TP8, FT10	6	P8, F7, T8, Fp2, TP10, P7, Fp1, FT10, O2, TP8	10
	Still noisy channels		0		0
	RANSAC	Fp2	1	FT9, POz, CPz	3
15	Noisy channels original	F2	1	F2, AFz, Fp2, AF7	4
	Interpolated channels	AF7	1	AF7	1
	Still noisy channels		0		0
	RANSAC	AF8	1	Fp1, Fp2, AF8	3
20	Noisy channels original	AF8, FT10, Fp2, AF7	4	AF8, Fp2, AF7, O2	4
	Interpolated channels	Fp2, AF8, FT10, AF7, TP10, FT9, TP9	7	O2, AF8, FT10, FT8, AF7, TP10, FT9, FT7	8
	Still noisy channels		0		0
	RANSAC	FC5, T7, F4, F5, AF4	5	FC5, F8, Fp2, AF3, F5, AF4	6
26	Noisy channels original	FC3, FCz, F1, AF4	4	FC3, C1, FCz, FC1, F1, AF4, Cz, FC6	8
	Interpolated channels	FC3, FC5, TP10, AF4, FT7	5	FC3, FCz, AF4, TP9	4
	Still noisy channels	FT9	1		0
	RANSAC	Cz, T8, FC6, AF7	4	T7, Cz, FC6, C1	4
29	Noisy channels original	FC4, AF3, F4, AF7, FC1, F7, F1, F8, AFz, F6	10	POz, Fp2, FC4, AF8, AF3, F4, AF7, Fp1, F7, F5, FC1, F1, F8, AFz, TP9, F6	16
	Interpolated channels	FC5, FC4, CP5, AF3, CP6, AF7, C5, PO4, FC6, FT9, F6	11	POz, FC4, AF8, CP5, FT7, AF7, F7, TP9, F6	9
	Still noisy channels		0		0
	RANSAC	P7, AF4	2	CP6, AF3, AF4	3
34	Noisy channels original	F2, TP8	2	TP8	1
	Interpolated channels	T8, TP8	2	T8, TP8	2
	Still noisy channels		0		0
	RANSAC	T7, AF3, FT7, AF8	4	Fp2, AF8	2
38	Noisy channels original	Fp2, AF8, AF7, Fp1, F1	5	Fp2, AF8, AF7, Fp1, F1, F8	6
	Interpolated channels	AF8, Fp2, AF7, Fp1	4	Fp2, AF8, T8, FT8, AF7, Fp1, F8	7
	Still noisy channels		0		0
	RANSAC	T7, TP9, P7, O1, TP10, T8, TP7, TP8, F6	9	P7, O1, FC6, C6	4

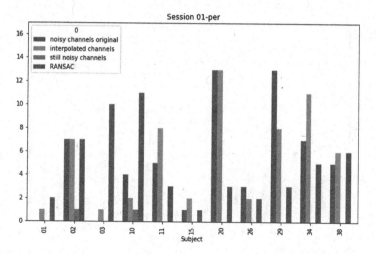

Fig. 4. Number of defective electrodes detected and interpolated in the perception task of session 1.

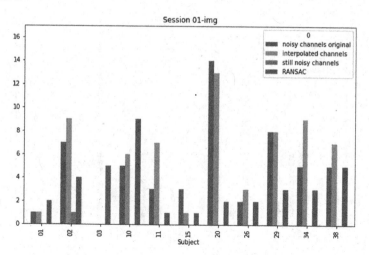

Fig. 5. Number of defective electrodes detected and interpolated in the imagery task of session 1.

The bar graphs show of Figs. 4, 5, 6, 7 the number of bad electrodes detected and interpolated for each session and task. The differences between PREP and *RANSAC*, and between subjects, can be seen. Both the tables and the bar graphs above show a similar trend in the detection of the bad electrodes between one task and another within the same session, and the differences between sessions (e.g., Subject 20), which could be an indication of a failure in the data collection within the session.

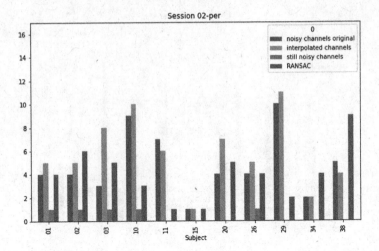

Fig. 6. Number of defective electrodes detected and interpolated in the perception task of session 2.

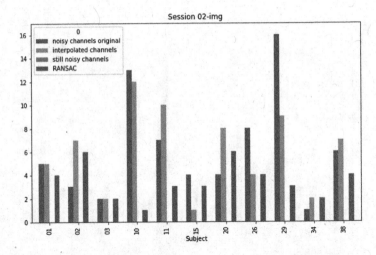

Fig. 7. Number of defective electrodes detected and interpolated in the imagery task of session 2.

The bar chart in Fig. 8 presents the epochs rejected for each session-task, taking into account that they start at 480 epochs. With respect to the analysis of epochs, the type of task does not seem to influence the quality of epochs, from an inter-subject comparison.

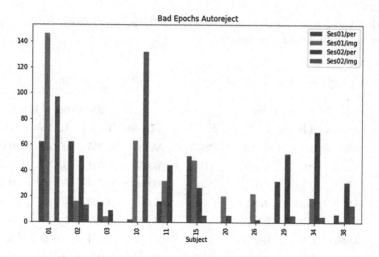

Fig. 8. Number of epochs rejected.

Tables 3 and 4 show the SNR for the 4 frequency bands in the perception and imagery tasks, respectively. When comparing the pre-processed data with the raw data, it is observed that the SNR after pipeline is higher than the raw data. It is also noticeable that the SNR improves much more in the perception task than in the imagination task, probably because of the nature of the perception task, the signal in the perception task is more distinguishable from the background noise. It is noteworthy that the greatest improvement is in the Alpha band in the

Table 3. SNR of the 4 bands for the perception task in the raw and pre-processed data.

Subject	Raw				Preprocesing			
	Alpha	Theta	L. Beta	H. Beta	Alpha	Theta	L. Beta	H. Beta
01	0.3	0.173	0.037	0.015	1.283	0.732	0.233	0.114
02	0.144	0.107	0.061	0.034	0.498	0.517	0.12	0.088
03	0.069	0.083	0.018	0.016	0.427	0.184	0.073	0.089
10	0.196	0.076	0.029	0.014	0.868	0.515	0.157	0.079
11	0.22	0.164	0.042	0.024	1.256	0.893	0.185	0.11
15	0.084	0.043	0.016	0.016	0.983	0.45	0.103	0.082
20	0.242	0.106	0.038	0.022	1.163	0.515	0.14	0.104
26	0.081	0.074	0.033	0.028	0.67	0.282	0.126	0.151
29	0.07	0.05	0.023	0.017	0.604	0.271	0.089	0.086
34	0.179	0.154	0.048	0.019	1.545	0.963	0.252	0.113
38	0.101	0.083	0.033	0.024	0.846	0.488	0.129	0.078

perception task, which is the band where [23] finds the greatest correspondence between perception and imagination.

Table 4. SNR of the 4 bands for the imagery task in the raw and pre-processed data.

Subject	Raw				Preprocesing			
	Alpha	Theta	L. Beta	H. Beta	Alpha	Theta	L. Beta	H. Beta
01	0.068	0.034	0.016	0.015	0.131	0.045	0.021	0.022
02	0.186	0.085	0.044	0.033	0.05	0.041	0.03	0.038
03	0.034	0.017	0.015	0.013	0.059	0.018	0.016	0.019
10	0.097	0.03	0.019	0.013	0.063	0.027	0.021	0.021
11	0.109	0.056	0.027	0.015	0.04	0.022	0.018	0.017
15	0.069	0.027	0.015	0.011	0.048	0.021	0.016	0.016
20	0.084	0.057	0.024	0.024	0.151	0.043	0.028	0.028
26	0.043	0.033	0.014	0.012	0.045	0.021	0.017	0.017
29	0.054	0.026	0.019	0.016	0.102	0.025	0.019	0.02
34	0.053	0.037	0.018	0.013	0.058	0.028	0.022	0.021
38	0.098	0.02	0.015	0.011	0.067	0.023	0.017	0.017

Taking as a reference the work in [23], where the *alpha* band is the band where the shared representations between visual perception and imagination are best presented, in this work we evaluate the *pipeline* with the results of 4 bands.

Figures 9, 10, 11, 12 presents the average of the decoding accuracy results in the MVPA with the imagination and visual perception data.

As can be seen, the *pipeline* achieves data representing similar temporal dynamics as obtained in [23]. This is due to robust rereferencing, enhanced channel detection and interpolation, and rejection of faulty epochs.

4   Conclusions

An essential step for EEG signal extraction is through an automatic and standardized preprocessing *pipeline* that efficiently facilitates feature extraction processes. As neuro signal research trends move to larger sample sizes, the traditional manual data rejection approach becomes untenable with higher density EEG channel designs. The proposed procedure combines preprocessing steps and provides higher quality data for research.

Generalization across time Alpha Train Perception-Imagery

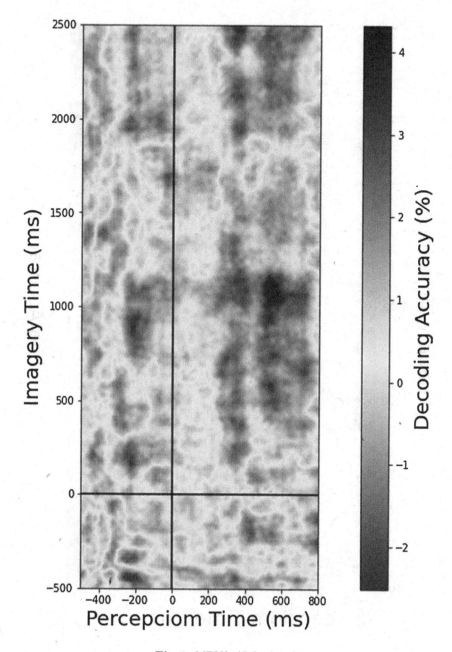

Fig. 9. MPVA Alpha band

Generalization across time Theta Train Perception-Imagery

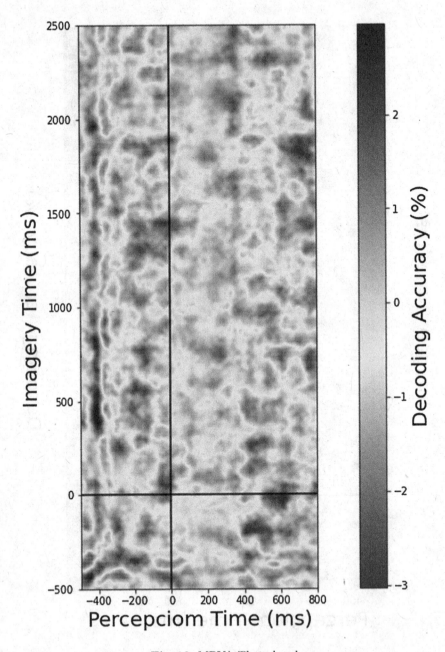

Fig. 10. MPVA Theta band

Generalization across time Low Beta Train Perception-Imagery

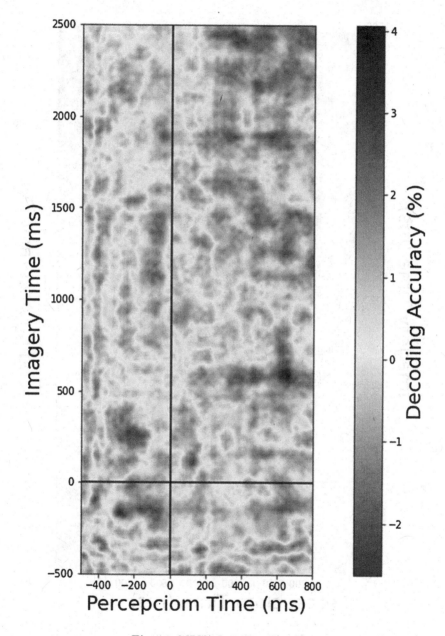

Fig. 11. MPVA Low Beta band

Generalization across time High Beta Train Perception-Imagery

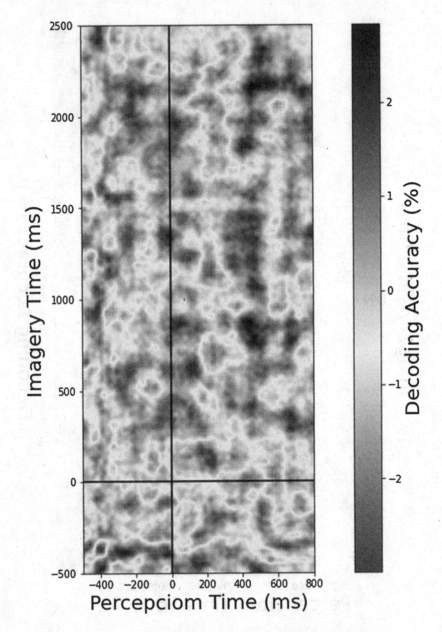

Fig. 12. MPVA High Beta band

While the preprocessing steps can be computationally expensive, this work demonstrates that systematic early identification and interpolation of channels and epochs with "non-EEG" behavior are important to improve the analysis results and provide the basis for data sharing to ensure reproducibility of the study.

On the other hand, to improve reproducibility, it is expected to add in the future to the *pipeline* the function of generating preprocessing reports by subject and study group. Additionally, it is necessary to include another process to define the number of SSP components, which is still being developed manually.

Acknowledgements. The authors would like to thank Siying Xie for her help in providing process details of their study on shared neural representations in the *alpha* frequency band.

References

1. Aggarwal, S., Chugh, N.: Signal processing techniques for motor imagery brain computer interface: a review. Array **1**, 100003 (2019). https://doi.org/10.1016/j.array.2019.100003
2. Andersson, P., Ragni, F., Lingnau, A.: Visual imagery during real-time fMRI neurofeedback from occipital and superior parietal cortex. Neuroimage **200**, 332–343 (2019). https://doi.org/10.1016/j.neuroimage.2019.06.057
3. Bigdely-Shamlo, N., Mullen, T., Kothe, C., Su, K.M., Robbins, K.A.: The PREP pipeline: standardized preprocessing for large-scale EEG analysis. Front. Neuroinform. **9**(JUNE), 1–19 (2015). https://doi.org/10.3389/fninf.2015.00016
4. Bobrov, P., Frolov, A., Cantor, C., Fedulova, I., Bakhnyan, M.: Brain-computer interface based on generation of visual images. PLoS ONE **6**(6), 20674 (2011). https://doi.org/10.1371/journal.pone.0020674, www.plosone.org
5. Combrisson, E., Jerbi, K.: Exceeding chance level by chance: the caveat of theoretical chance levels in brain signal classification and statistical assessment of decoding accuracy. J. Neurosci. Meth. **250**, 126–136 (2015). https://doi.org/10.1016/j.jneumeth.2015.01.010
6. Díez, Á., Suazo, V., Casado, P., Martín-Loeches, M., Molina, V.: Spatial distribution and cognitive correlates of gamma noise power in schizophrenia. Psychol. Med. **43**(6), 1175–1185 (2013). https://doi.org/10.1017/S0033291712002103, https://www.cambridge.org/core/journals/psychological-medicine/article/abs/spatial-distribution-and-cognitive-correlates-of-gamma-noise-power-in-schizophrenia/0CF52AD2D5BC981285F61F7A901ADD00
7. Dijkstra, N., Zeidman, P., Ondobaka, S., Van Gerven, M.A., Friston, K.: Distinct top-down and bottom-up brain connectivity during visual perception and imagery. Sci. Rep. **7**(1), 1–9 (2017). https://doi.org/10.1038/s41598-017-05888-8
8. Dijkstra, N., Bosch, S.E., Van Gerven, M.A.J.: Shared neural mechanisms of visual perception and imagery. Trends Cogn. Sci. **23**, 423–434 (2019). https://doi.org/10.1016/j.tics.2019.02.004
9. Esfahani, E.T., Sundararajan, V.: Classification of primitive shapes using brain–computer interfaces. Comput. Aided Des. **44**, 1011–1019 (2012). https://doi.org/10.1016/j.cad.2011.04.008, www.elsevier.com/locate/cad

10. Fulford, J., et al.: The neural correlates of visual imagery vividness - an fMRI study and literature review. Cortex **105**, 26–40 (2018). https://doi.org/10.1016/j.cortex.2017.09.014

11. Winterer, G., et al.: Schizophrenia: reduced signal-to-noise ratio and impaired phase-locking during information processing. Clin. Neurophysiol. Off. J. Int. Fed. Clin. Neurophysiol. **111**(5), 837–849 (2000). https://doi.org/10.1016/S1388-2457(99)00322-3, https://pubmed.ncbi.nlm.nih.gov/10802455/

12. Gabard-Durnam, L.J., Mendez Leal, A.S., Wilkinson, C.L., Levin, A.R.: The Harvard Automated Processing Pipeline for Electroencephalography (HAPPE): standardized processing software for developmental and high-artifact data. Front. Neurosci. **12**, 97 (2018). https://doi.org/10.3389/fnins.2018.00097

13. Gramfort, A.: MEG and EEG data analysis with MNE-Python. Front. Neurosci. **7**, 267 (2013). https://doi.org/10.3389/fnins.2013.00267

14. Jas, M., Engemann, D.A., Bekhti, Y., Raimondo, F., Gramfort, A.: Autoreject: automated artifact rejection for MEG and EEG data. Neuroimage **159**, 417–429 (2017). https://doi.org/10.1016/j.neuroimage.2017.06.030

15. Jas, M., et al.: A reproducible MEG/EEG group study with the MNE software: recommendations, quality assessments, and good practices. Front. Neurosci. **12**(AUG), 530 (2018). https://doi.org/10.3389/fnins.2018.00530

16. Keogh, R., Pearson, J.: The perceptual and phenomenal capacity of mental imagery. Cognition **162**, 124–132 (2017). https://doi.org/10.1016/j.cognition.2017.02.004

17. Lawhern, V.J., Solon, A.J., Waytowich, N.R.: A review of classification algorithms for EEG-based brain-computer interfaces: a 10 year update. J. Neural Eng. **15**, 031005 (2018). https://doi.org/10.1088/1741-2552/aab2f2

18. Lee, S.H., Lee, M., Jeong, J.H., Lee, S.W.: Towards an EEG-based intuitive BCI communication system using imagined speech and visual imagery. In: Conference Proceedings - IEEE International Conference on Systems, Man and Cybernetics 2019-October, pp. 4409–4414 (2019). https://doi.org/10.1109/SMC.2019.8914645

19. Levin, A.R., Méndez Leal, A.S., Gabard-Durnam, L.J., O'Leary, H.M.: BEAPP: the Batch Electroencephalography Automated Processing Platform. Front. Neurosci. **12**(AUG), 513 (2018). https://doi.org/10.3389/fnins.2018.00513

20. Pearson, J., Naselaris, T., Holmes, E.A., Kosslyn, S.M.: Mental imagery: functional mechanisms and clinical applications. Trends Cogn. Sci. **19**(10), 590–602 (2015). https://doi.org/10.1016/j.tics.2015.08.003, https://linkinghub.elsevier.com/retrieve/pii/S1364661315001801

21. Perrin, F., Pernier, J., Bertrand, O., Echallier, J.F.: Spherical splines for scalp potential and current density mapping. Electroencephalogr. Clin. Neurophysiol. **72**(2), 184–187 (1989). https://doi.org/10.1016/0013-4694(89)90180-6

22. Suarez-Perez, A., et al.: Quantification of signal-to-noise ratio in cerebral cortex recordings using flexible MEAs with co-localized platinum black, carbon nanotubes, and gold electrodes. Front. Neurosci. **0**(NOV), 862 (2018). https://doi.org/10.3389/FNINS.2018.00862

23. Xie, S., Kaiser, D., Cichy, R.M.: Visual imagery and perception share neural representations in the alpha frequency band. Curr. Biol. **30**(13), 2621–2627.e5 (2020). https://doi.org/10.1016/j.cub.2020.04.074

Multilabel and Multiclass Approaches Comparison for Respiratory Sounds Classification

Andrés Felipe Romero Gómez[(✉)] and Alvaro D. Orjuela-Cañón

Universidad del Rosario, Bogotá, D.C, Colombia
andresfe.romero@urosario.edu.com

Abstract. Respiratory diseases are one of the leading causes of death worldwide according to ten World Health Organization (WHO) due to fatal issues and produce a decreasing of the life quality for people who suffer it. Therefore, there is a necessity to generate tools that allow agile and reliable diagnostic support systems for management of these diseases. Recently, different approaches based on artificial intelligence (AI), mostly at employing artificial neural networks (NN) have been validated to be a successful alternative in respiratory diseases diagnosis using images and signals as information sources. The present proposal uses AI algorithms used on auscultation signals from the respiratory system, identifying respiratory sounds associated to pulmonary diseases (crackles and wheezes). The records used were extracted from the Respiratory Sound Database of the ICBHI 2017 Challenge. Different works have used this database to apply a multiclass classification with satisfactory performance results. However, the ICBHI holds the labels in a multilabel format. Due to this, the present work explores the use of the multilabel target for the classification of these respiratory sounds. Statistics from time and frequency features were used to train five classic machine learning (ML) models for a comparison between multilabel and multiclass classification. A k-fold cross-validation was employed to evaluate the performance of the models with similar results compared to the classical multiclass classification, but with the advantages of the multilabel employment objective such as better represents the problem, make it a better alternative.

Keywords: Respiratory sound classification · Machine learning · Signal processing · Diagnosis support system

1 Introduction

Respiratory diseases, such as chronic obstructive pulmonary disease (COPD) and other infectious diseases are among the leading causes of death worldwide, according to a report by the World Health Organization (WHO) [1]. In addition, the life quality of people with these diseases is reduced due to a lower respiratory capacity that makes unable to develop a comfortable life. In this way, new and alternative methods to speed up and reliable diagnosis of respiratory diseases are essential for early and effective treatment, making the difference for this kind of diseases [2, 3].

© Springer Nature Switzerland AG 2022
A. D. Orjuela-Cañón et al. (Eds.): ColCACI 2021, CCIS 1471, pp. 53–62, 2022.
https://doi.org/10.1007/978-3-030-91308-3_4

One of the most important procedures employed to evaluate the respiratory system is the auscultation, which consists of listening to internal sounds of the body, mainly the airways and lungs, to assess whether there are normal or pathological sounds. The low cost and common use of the auscultation contribute to more technologies based on this procedure may be included and accepted as part of the physicians' workflow. However, there is a wide discussion about the diagnostic accuracy of this method, since the lung auscultation has a low sensitivity in different clinical settings and patient populations [4]. In addition, there is evidence related to the high variability in these specific respiratory sounds, which can be affected by factors such as gender, body size, subject position, and location of auscultation can provide confusing information [4]. Despite this, the auscultation process is useful because lung sounds convey relevant information for pulmonary disorders, including adventitious sounds (AS) such as wheezes and crackles, overlapping with normal respiration [5].

Wheezes sounds are continuous AS related to obstructive airways pathologies and can determine the severity and the respiratory issues location. The asthma and respiratory stenosis are the most common pathologies studied through wheezes sound analysis. Typically, wheezes can have frequencies between 100 Hz and 2500 Hz, with a time period duration of intervals between 50 ms and 250 ms [6]. On the other hand, crackles sounds are related to shorter and more explosive behavior, associated to diseases such as lung infections, pneumonia, pulmonary edema, and others. For these specific AS, time duration and frequency domain characteristics depend on the pathology [6, 7].

Developing countries have difficulties in their healthcare systems, such as a lack of trained personnel and the required infrastructure, especially in territories far away from the most important cities. In addition, the low indexes of air quality increase the risk factor of getting respiratory diseases such as COPD [8, 9]. Finally, another adversity in these regions is associated to the precarious health infrastructure, which does not have laboratories or adequate consulting rooms. These aspects make necessary more alternatives that can support the health professionals work related to diagnosis tasks.

In recent years, artificial intelligence (AI) and a subfield as machine learning (ML) have been used in medicine to develop decision support systems (DSS). DSS have the purpose to provide additional information, where the physicians can make better decisions based on a suggestion from an AI model, which in some tasks can outperform experts [10, 11]. Also, front-line healthcare workers can employ DSS to reduce the workload as a benefit, and in some cases, having a low cost of implementation and improving the decision making [12, 13].

Employing AI techniques, some works have determined wheezes and crackles from respiratory sounds by performing a multiclass classification, either for two classes: normal or AS, or for four classes: normal, wheezing, crackles, or the presence of both [14–16]. For feature extraction stage, spectrograms or components that represent the entire signal in a single vector were employed. In addition, many authors have used the Mel-spectrum frequency strategy [14], or the employment of the short-time Fourier transform (STFT) to compute the spectrograms and the use of Convolutional Neural Networks (CNNs) in the classification stage [15]. Another strategy for the signal representation is based on time and frequency features calculated through small time windows (short-term features, STF), and statistics measures calculations as mean and standard deviation of these STF, known as Long-Term Features (LTFs) and employ classic ML models [17]. Different ML algorithms have been used and the results have been reported, comparing artificial neural networks (ANN), support vector machines (SVM), linear discriminant analysis (LDA), and other strategies to classify AS respiratory signals, using different methods for feature extraction [5, 14, 18]. However, the reached performance of the presented models, based on mentioned feature extraction techniques, holds accuracy values upper than 90%, but requiring the use of complex computational models as CNN to classify just crackles events and non-crackles ones.

In this work, a multilabel approach is used and compared to multiclass classification according to the output implementation of the ML models. In multilabel classification, the presence of crackles and wheezes in the same cycle is not an independent class, so models can use these instances to improve their performance in classifying wheezes and crackles. Long time feature (LTF) extraction was used as the method to represent each respiratory cycle. As a classification stage, five ML models where implemented: ANN, random forest (RF), support vector machines (SVM), logistic regression (LR), and k-nearest neighbor (KNN). ANN, RF, and KNN support multilabel and multiclass classification and LR and SVM only support multiclass classification. The records used are from the Respiratory Sound Database of the ICBHI 2017 Challenge, which has annotations for each respiratory cycle and information about the presence or absence of crackles and wheezes.

2 Materials and Methods

Figure 1 shows an overview of the implemented methodology. First, audio files were extracted from the Respiratory Sound Database of the International Conference on Biomedical Health Informatics - ICBHI 2017 [6]. The database was built from 5.5 h of recordings, obtaining 6898 respiratory cycles registers: 1864 crackles and 886 wheezes, and 506 both crackles and wheezes. For this, 920 audio samples were annotated from 126 subjects with a provided diagnosis related to respiratory diseases. Particular aspects of the database correspond to recording, due to the signals of the respiratory sounds were taken at different chest locations, and with different acquisition systems.

A first step based on signals normalization was developed, where each respiratory cycle was taken as reference. The feature extraction stage was obtained using LTF from small time windows. Finally, ML models were proposed and validated through the k-fold cross-validation method.

2.1 Preprocessing

The respiratory cycles were resampled at 4 kHz for normalization of all records since the devices used to record the auscultation signals have different sampling frequencies. After resampling, each cycle signal was normalized by the absolute maximum value, and short length cycles were removed due to not physiologically possibility. Then, only respiratory cycles with length longer than 1 s were considered.

In the dataset, each respiratory cycle has a multilabel target with two values. One of them corresponds to the presence of wheezes, and the other one to the presence of

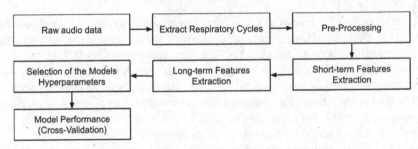

Fig. 1. General scheme of the methodology.

crackles. The multilabel target allows casting the labels to four classes (normal, crackles, wheezes, and crackles and wheezes), and two classes (normal, abnormal sounds). The three types of labeling were used to train and test the models.

2.2 Feature Extraction

For feature extraction, STF were extracted from windows of 50ms and 50% of overlapping. For each window, a computation of 13 MFCCs coefficients was followed: the zero-crossing rate, the root mean square, a spectral roll-off of 10% and 90%, and the spectral centroid. The Librosa Python library was employed for this task [19], obtaining STF for each cycle and the computation of mean and standard deviation to calculate the LTF. In this way, each respiratory cycle was represented by a vector with 36 components produced by the described procedure. Figure 2 shows a diagram of the preprocessing and feature extraction procedure.

After preprocessing and feature extraction, the number of samples was 6596, 1829 for crackles, 858 for wheezes, 503 for crackles and wheezes in the same cycle, and 3406 samples from normal breath. As mentioned, each sample was represented 36 features for each respiratory cycle, and a normalization in the interval $[-1, 1]$.

2.3 Experimental Setup

The main objective of the present work is to develop a multilabel classification, comparing to the multiclass approach. Therefore, three classification strategies were used: two-classes, four-classes and multilabel classifications. The classification for two and four classes was implemented by five ML models: KNN, LR, SVM, ANN, and RF. The multilabel classification was performed by KNN, ANN, and RF models due to the limitations of the representation of the labels in the output. These last models can learn from two labels in the output, simultaneously. An example of this is the ANN, where two neurons (corresponding to two different outputs) were used to compute the error and back-propagate it through the network.

ML models were trained to perform the three types of classification when it was possible, to compare the performance between the different approaches. In the comparison, the output of models trained for multilabel classification was adapted to two-class and four-class outputs. The output of the models trained for four-class classification was transformed to two-class output. Finally, the models trained to classify between normal

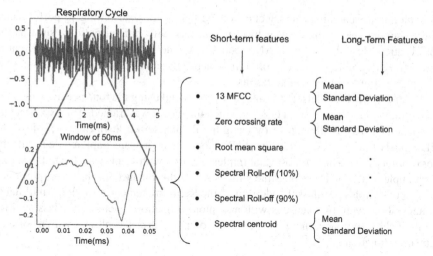

Fig. 2. Diagram of the preprocessing and feature extraction process.

respiratory cycles and cycles with AS were not modified due to the few information available to implement it.

The model's hyperparameters exploration was followed by a data division into 20% for training and 80% for testing. This because the idea of the exploration was to reduce the search space of the best hyperparameters. A k-fold cross-validation with 5-folds was employed to find the hyperparameters that achieve the best results in predicting new data. The folds were stratified for preserving the percentage of samples for each class. Figure 3 shows an overview of the experimental setup, according to the implemented classifications.

The performance evaluation was based on the accuracy of the classification types: i) Accuracy for the two-class classification, which can be obtained from all the models. ii) Accuracy for the four-class classification, where models trained for the two-class classification were not evaluated. iii) Average accuracy (Av. Acc) computed from the accuracy of the prediction of wheezes and crackles as two different outputs for the multilabel classification models. iv) Accuracy over all labels (Acc. labels) predictions for the multilabel classification case. In iv), it was considered that the prediction from the multilabel model was not completely wrong, since the classes were not mutually exclusive, and for one instance it was possible to classify correctly two, one, or no outputs. In addition, in i) and ii), the accuracy was balanced, according to the number of samples for each class, considering that the database is imbalanced.

For stabilizing the imbalanced effect, the models were trained taking into account the number of samples in each one. In this way, the class imbalance existing in the dataset is adjusted inversely proportional to class frequencies in the training data. For the KNN model, there was no such class balance, due to this implies considering the distances between samples to give more importance to near samples. On the other hand, the numerical hyperparameters such as the regularization parameter (C) in LR and SVM, or the number of neighbors for the KNN model (n neighbors), were determined from an exploration, searching the selection of the best values, according to performance in the training set. In the case of hyperparameters with limited options, such as the optimization algorithm used in ANN and LR, or the type of kernel in SVM, entire alternative possibilities were explored. In general, these last hyperparameters were the variables that more influence the results.

For the five ML models, the results were compared using the four-accuracy metrics, depending on the classification task for which the model was trained. The experimental computations were implemented by using the Python sci-kit-learn library [20] for the ML models training, excluding the ANN models which were implemented with the Keras library [21]. This ANN special implementation with Keras was due to the sci-kit learn implementation is not possible with class weights balance for the disproportioned number of samples per class. In addition, in the Keras implementation for the multilabel strategy, there were two neurons with a sigmoid activation function per class, and for the multiclass approach, there were as many output neurons as classes with a softmax activation function.

3   Results and Discussion

Table 1 shows the hyperparameters with best results for every classification strategy, according to each ML model. As mentioned, the hyperparameters related to optimization algorithm in the ANN, LR and SVM, and type of kernel in SVM, had the most influence for the results.

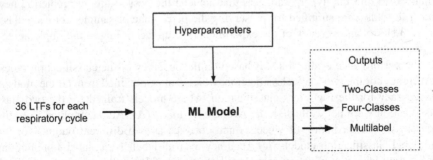

Fig. 3. Overview of the experimental Setup.

Table 2 shows the accuracy for the two-class classification models. For the four-class classification, Table 3 presents the accuracy for the employed models. Finally, Table 4 exhibits the accuracy for all the classification strategies for the models trained for the multilabel approach, with highlighted values (letters in bold) for the best results. The KNN model obtained the best performance for every one of the classification strategies. This model differs from the others since it does not attempt to construct an internal model with an optimization process. KNN only stores the instances of the trained data and classifies the instances using a majority vote of the nearest neighbors of each point representation. Each point was created in the feature space from the 36 LTFs. This

Table 1. Best hyperparameters for each ML algorithm.

ML Model	Hyperparameters
KNN	algorithm = ball tree leaf size = 30 n neighbors = 2 weights = distance
LR	C = 300 solver = lbfgs class weight = balanced
SVM	C = 120 gama = scale kernel = rbf class weight = balanced
ANN	number of neurons in hidden layer = 183 hidden layer activation function = relu learning rate = 0.001 batch size = 60 class weight = balanced validation split = 0.1 early stopping = 50
RF	criterion = gini max features = auto min samples split = 23 n estimators = 120 class weight = balanced

allowed to infer that this representation from the LFTs was enough to do the classification of the respiratory cycles.

Comparing the results for multiclass and multilabel approaches, there were no significant differences in the accuracies for the multiclass classification. However, the multilabel metrics show that it is possible to train models using this strategy with comparable results to the multiclass classification (see Table 4). Additionally, multilabel targets have the advantage of being more realistic since the respiratory cycles with crackles, wheezes and, wheezes and crackles, are not mutually exclusive.

Table 2. Performance of all the models trained for the two-class classification task.

ML model	Two-class accuracy
KNN	**82.05 ± 0.85%**
LR	64.98 ± 0.97%
SVM	78.03 ± 1.22%
ANN	69.33 ± 1.76%
RF	76.42 ± 1.12%

Table 3. Performance of all the models trained for the four-class classification task.

ML model	Two-class accuracy	Four-class accuracy
KNN	**82.05 ± 0.85%**	**68.31 ± 1.65%**
LR	63.35 ± 1.04%	46.30 ± 0.98%
SVM	76.94 ± 1.21%	64.75 ± 1.18%
ANN	66.34 ± 4.67%	38.88 ± 4.17%
RF	74.20 ± 1.64%	58.07 ± 1.54%

Table 4. Performance of the models with the multilabel classification strategy.

ML model	Two-class accuracy	Four-class accuracy	Av. acc	Av. labels
KNN	**82.05 ± 0.85%**	**68.31 ± 1.65%**	**82.48 ± 1.08%**	**86.06 ± 0.66%**
ANN	66.99 ± 3.05%	41.39 ± 3.33%	64.10 ± 2.84%	77.04 ± 1.47%
RF	73.77 ± 1.46%	56.23 ± 0.99%	74.75 ± 0.49%	81.45 ± 0.66%

On the other hand, in Tables 2, 3, and 4, there were large differences in the accuracy of the four classes. Some models achieved accuracies greater than 64% as minimum performance (see Table 2), and others more than 39% as minimum (see Table 3). That is because the models were taking advantage of class imbalance and setting the class weight equal to balanced was not enough. Moreover, these results compared to other works are apparently worse, for example, in [11] the reported four-class and two-class accuracies were 78.4% and 83.7% respectively. There, the accuracy calculated did not consider the balanced classes, according to this information was not included in the work. If the calculated accuracy for the KNN model was not balanced for the model trained in the multilabel task, the four-class accuracy could be 75.16%, instead of 68.31%. This evinces the necessity of using the balanced accuracy to obtain a better estimate of model performance.

Looking for an alternative that employs fewer features, the multilabel models were trained with the LTFs from the 13 MFCCs. Table 5 exhibits the results of training the models for the multilabel task in the test subsets. It is possible to see that there were no significant differences between using the 26 features from the MFCCs and all set of 36 features.

Table 5. Performance of the models with the multilabel classification strategy using only MFCCs.

ML model	Two-class accuracy	Four-class accuracy	Av. acc	Av. labels
KNN	82.20 ± 0.41%	68.10 ± 1.08%	82.50 ± 0.82%	86.02 ± 0.49%
ANN	66.99 ± 3.05%	41.39 ± 3.33%	64.10 ± 2.84%	77.04 ± 1.47%
RF	73.82 ± 1.54%	55.46 ± 1.41%	74.45 ± 1.18%	80.88 ± 1.19%

Comparing the present results to the literature reports, and employing the same database [6], a first work obtained the highest benchmark value during the contest, reaching 49.86% for accuracy [12]. More recent works have reported results of 85% in accuracy for two classes (healthy patients and patients with respiratory symptoms), employing 330 features and an ANN [16]. Furthermore, results by using Mel spectrum and a CNN reached 87.3% in sensitivity and 69.4% for specificity, obtaining comparable values to the present proposal [14]. Finally, other works just reached values lower than 65% in the accuracy for four classes and more complex ANN architectures [15].

4 Conclusions

This paper presented a comparison between training ML models for multilabel and multiclass classification of AS. The trained models obtained comparable results to similar works, and no significant differences were found in the use of both classification strategies. However, the use of the multilabel target had advantages related to a better approximation for realistic representation of the problem. Furthermore, it was found that it is necessary to use performance metrics that consider the class imbalance in the database, allowing the models to learn properly, in spite of the imbalance sample quantities.

Another particular aspect of this work is associated to the employment of classical ML models, which even with the possibility of using deep learning models, such as CNNs, the ML models do not require large databases or high computational costs for training. At the same time, it was found that similar results can be obtained using only 13 MFCCs compared to use the entire features set. The importance of low computational cost lies in the software and hardware that must be used for implementation. For this reason, the development of simple models with good performance can help to make the technology more accessible for healthcare applications.

References

1. Rana, J.S., Khan, S.S., Lloyd-Jones, D.M., Sidney, S.: Changes in mortality in top 10 causes of death from 2011 to 2018. J. Gen. Intern. Med. **36**, 2517–2518 (2021)
2. Dou, M., Macias, N., Shen, F., Bard, J.D., Dom'inguez, D.C., Li, X.: Rapid and accurate diagnosis of the respiratory disease pertussis on a point-of-care biochip. EClinicalMed. **8**, 72–77 (2019)
3. Zhang, N., et al.: Recent advances in the detection of respiratory virus infection in humans. J. Med. Virol. **92**, 408–417 (2020)
4. Arts, L., Lim, E.H.T., van de Ven, P.M., Heunks, L., Tuinman, P.R.: The diagnostic accuracy of lung auscultation in adult patients with acute pulmonary pathologies: a meta-analysis. Sci. Rep. **10**, 1–11 (2020)
5. Pramono, R.X.A., Bowyer, S., Rodriguez-Villegas, E.: Automatic adventitious respiratory sound analysis: a systematic review. PLoS ONE **12**, e0177926 (2017)
6. Rocha, B.M., et al.: A respiratory sound database for the development of automated classification. In: Maglaveras, N., Chouvarda, I., de Carvalho, P. (eds.) Precision Medicine Powered by pHealth and Connected Health: ICBHI 2017, Thessaloniki, Greece, 18-21 November 2017, pp. 33–37. Springer Singapore, Singapore (2018). https://doi.org/10.1007/978-981-10-741 9-6_6

7. Orjuela-Cañón, A.D., Gómez-Cajas, D.F., Jiménez-Moreno, R.: Artificial neural networks for acoustic lung signals classification. In: Bayro-Corrochano, E., Hancock, E. (eds.) CIARP 2014. LNCS, vol. 8827, pp. 214–221. Springer, Cham (2014). https://doi.org/10.1007/978-3-319-12568-8_27
8. Viegi, G., Maio, S., Fasola, S., Baldacci, S.: Global burden of chronic respiratory diseases. J. Aerosol Med. Pulm. Drug Deliv. **33**, 171–177 (2020)
9. Quaderi, S.A., Hurst, J.R.: The unmet global burden of COPD. Global Health, Epidemiol. Genom. **3**, e4 (2018). https://doi.org/10.1017/gheg.2018.1
10. Shortliffe, E.H., Sepúlveda, M.J.: Clinical decision support in the era of artificial intelligence. JAMA **320**, 2199–2200 (2018)
11. Chen, M., Decary, M.: Artificial intelligence in healthcare: an essential guide for health leaders. Healthcare Manag. Forum **33**(1), 10–18 (2020). https://doi.org/10.1177/084047041 9873123
12. Amisha, P.M., Pathania, M., Rathaur, V.K.: Overview of artificial intelligence in medicine. J. Fam. Med. Prim. Care. **8**, 2328 (2019)
13. Panch, T., Szolovits, P., Atun, R.: Artificial intelligence, machine learning and health systems. J. Glob. Health. **8** (2018)
14. Chambres, G., Hanna, P., Desainte-Catherine, M.: Automatic detection of patient with respiratory diseases using lung sound analysis. In: 2018 International Conference on Content-Based Multimedia Indexing (CBMI), pp. 1–6 (2018)
15. Nguyen, T., Pernkopf, F.: Lung sound classification using snapshot ensemble of convolutional neural networks. In: 2020 42nd Annual International Conference of the IEEE Engineering in Medicine & Biology Society (EMBC), pp. 760–763 (2020)
16. Ma, Y., Xu, X., Yu, Q., Zhang, Y., Li, Y., Zhao, J., Wang, G.: LungBRN: a smart digital stethoscope for detecting respiratory disease using bi-resnet deep learning algorithm. In: 2019 IEEE Biomedical Circuits and Systems Conference (BioCAS). pp. 1–4 (2019)
17. Monaco, A., Amoroso, N., Bellantuono, L., Pantaleo, E., Tangaro, S., Bellotti, R.: Multi-time-scale features for accurate respiratory sound classification. Appl. Sci. **10**, 8606 (2020)
18. Rocha, B.M., Pessoa, D., Marques, A., Carvalho, P., Paiva, R.P.: Automatic classification of adventitious respiratory sounds: a (un) solved problem? Sensors **21**, 57 (2021)
19. McFee, B., Raffel, C., Liang, D., Ellis, D.P.W., McVicar, M., Battenberg, E., Nieto, O.: Librosa: audio and music signal analysis in python. In: Proceedings of the 14th Python in Science Conference. pp. 18–25 (2015)
20. Pedregosa, F., et al.: Scikit-learn: machine learning in python. J. Mach. Learn. Res. **12**, 2825–2830 (2011)
21. Chollet, F., et al.: Keras. https://github.com/fchollet/keras (2015)

Alternative Proposals and Its Applications

Weighted Hausdorff Distance Loss as a Function of Different Metrics in Convolutional Neural Networks for Ladybird Beetle Detection

Mateo Vega[1], Diego S. Benítez[1]([✉]), Noel Pérez[1], Daniel Riofrío[1], Giovani Ramón[2], and Diego Cisneros-Heredia[2]

[1] Colegio de Ciencias e Ingenierías "El Politécnico", Universidad San Francisco de Quito USFQ, Quito 170157, Ecuador
mvega1@alumni.usfq.edu.ec, {dbenitez,nperez,driofrioa}@usfq.edu.ec
[2] Colegio de Ciencias Biológicas y Ambientales "COCIBA", Universidad San Francisco de Quito USFQ, Quito 170157, Ecuador
{gramonc,dcisneros}@usfq.edu.ec

Abstract. This work compares five different distance metrics (i.e., Euclidean, Chebyshev, Manhattan, Mahalanobis, and Canberra) implemented in the weighted Hausdorff distance (WHD) as part of the loss function during the training and validation of a fully convolutional neural network (FCNN) model for detecting ladybird beetle specimens. The FCNN-based detector was trained and validated using a ten-fold cross-validation method on a database composed of 2,633 wildlife images with ladybird beetles. The obtained results highlighted the Chebyshev metric as the top performer given a diverse dataset as ours. This metric scored the highest values in three out of four validation metrics (i.e., precision, recall, and F1-score). The nature of this metric allows substantial space for minimizing the cost function along the FCNN training step. Euclidean and Manhattan distances also provide good performance based on our validation metrics, while Mahalanobis and Canberra distances are not suitable for detecting of ladybird beetles.

Keywords: Ladybird beetle detection · Deep learning · Fully convolutional neural network · Weighted Hausdorff distance · Heat map

1 Introduction

Ladybird beetles are members of the *Coccinellidae* family and are among the top predators in terrestrial invertebrate communities. Several species of ladybugs have been deliberately translocated as biological control agents in America, Europe, and Africa since the beginning of the 20th century, establishing naturally and expanding global populations, becoming invasive [3]. These organisms

---

Work funded by Universidad San Francisco de Quito (USFQ) through the Collaboration Grants (Grant no. 16870) Program.

A. D. Orjuela-Cañón et al. (Eds.): ColCACI 2021, CCIS 1471, pp. 65–77, 2022.
https://doi.org/10.1007/978-3-030-91308-3_5

play essential ecosystem roles, and introduced *Coccinellidae* species can have several potentially important impacts on biological communities and ecosystem functions and economical impact for agricultural businesses if they establish a successful non-native population.

Ladybugs are voracious predators of agricultural pests, consuming soft body insects as essential prey, that is, aphids, coccidia, psyllids, and thin [12]. However, many species of invasive ladybugs have a range of dietary. They are polyphagous predators, consuming immature stages of other beetles, butterflies, flies, mites, and plant material, such as fruits, pollen, nectar, leaves, and seeds [26]. Invasive species of ladybugs seem to dominate confrontations with other ladybug species (predominantly native species), exercising intense predation pressure [9]. Due to their polyphagia and union interactions, non-native populations have adverse effects on native biodiversity and agribusiness by attacking non-target arthropods, modifying the structure and dynamics of the assemblages of invertebrates, replacing or marginalizing native *coccinellidae* by competition and predation, and feeding on harmful commercial fruits or agricultural products [26].

In this sense, three species of invasive ladybugs have recently significant expansions in Ecuador: *Harmonia axyridis*, *Mulsantina mexicana* and *Cheilomenes sexmaculata*. Despite its potential impacts, little information is available on the populations of these clades in Ecuador and even less in the Galapagos, archipelago with several species of native and endemic ladybugs, and where agricultural pests have become problematic, both for their ecological and agricultural impact. In particular, *Harmony axyridis* is classified among the 100 worst invasive species due to the potential of its impacts, being an invasive successful due to its wide dietary range, its ability to settle, disperse, and robustness and flexibility of its immune system [8,9,13].

Currently, the detection and classification of these invasive species occur by capturing a sample, and then specialists conduct its subsequently taxonomic analysis. This action model is entirely manual and requires time to obtain the specimen identification. Therefore, the implementation of an automated detection and classification approach would contribute to improving the control of these invasive species, and consequently to minimize the problems of ecological impact and agriculture in territories with great biodiversity (e.g. Galapagos archipelago).

Lately, deep learning techniques such as convolutional neural networks (CNN) have achieved remarkable results in detecting objects in images. Thus, there is a great potential of using CNNs in the automatic detection and classification of insects [10]. For example CNNs where used to estimate honeybee posture [20], distinguish between pollen-bearing and non-bearing honeybees [22], monitor interactions of honeybees in a hive [2], counting [17] and to tracking individual honeybees among wildflower clusters [15]. Regarding beetles detection, in [1] a contour-based image localization with reformed SqueezeNet transfer learning approach was used to classify tiger beetles of Sri Lanka, while in [23], a CNN based VGG16 model was used to create an easy solution to automated image-based taxon identification that was used to identify beetles including ladybird beetles in Sweden. Whereas, in [25] a two-step automatic detector for ladybird beetles in random environment images was proposed. First, saliency maps are used with simple linear iterative clustering superpixels segmentation and active contour methods to generate bounding boxes of possible ladybird beetles locations within an image. Then, a deep CNN-based classifier is used to select only the bounding boxes with ladybird beetles as the final output. This approach achieved a detection accuracy score of 92% in the used dataset.

Despite these developments, we found that automatic detection and classification of ladybird beetles in natural scenarios remain challenging. Therefore the use of deep learning techniques such as CNNs may be helpful. However, before the ladybird species can be recognized, accurate detection of a ladybird beetle within an image or video stream is needed. Once the ladybird beetle is detected, a region of interest (ROI) can be extracted, and then features can be used to recognize to what species it belongs. In this regard, object detection using CNNs has usually been done using a large number of anchor boxes like in Fast R-CNN [7], and YOLO [16] approaches. Recently, Ribera et al. [18] highlighted that the use of anchor boxes is unnecessary when the primary purpose is to detect the object itself instead of the surrounding area. They proposed representing an object in the image as a ground truth point, reducing the required time for the data annotation.

This paper proposes a comparative analysis of five different distance metrics implemented in the weighted Hausdorff distance (WHD) as part of the loss function during the training and validation of a fully convolutional neural network (FCNN) model for detecting ladybird beetle specimens. The FCNN model was developed in [18] and previously adapted to detect ladybird beetle samples in [24] with successful results. The main contributions behind this goal are related to answering if the FCNN architecture can be accurately used to detect ladybird beetles using only points of interest in images. Also, to discover if the Euclidean metric (used by default by the WHD function in the FCNN model) is the most suitable metric to implement in the WHD function for the problem under analysis. Moreover, this work constitutes another step towards developing robust ladybird beetle detectors that can be used in the future by a complete automated system to identify and classify different invasive ladybird species.

2   Materials and Methods

2.1   Database

A ladybird beetle image database was taken from the *iNaturalist*[1] project, which is a citizen-based science effort that lets the general public pool their observations on an online social network (the *iNaturalist* website) using an app. Within the *iNaturalist* project, biodiversity information about observations of different plant and animal species is documented by the general public and specialists worldwide

---

[1] *iNaturalist* project is provided by courtesy of the California Academy of Sciences and the National Geographic Society, and it is available at http://www.inaturalist.org.

to help each other learn about nature. Data can be filtered and downloaded according to the needs.

For our purposes, we only assembled a database with ladybird beetle observations from Ecuador and Colombia regions. Only images labeled as "research-grade" were selected, which means that experts within the *iNaturalist* project have verified the observations. Each image was also individually inspected to confirm correct family identification and keep only adult ladybird beetle samples. Adult ladybird beetles have clear external morphology and coloration patterns, which ease their identification by humans in random wildlife images. Hence, the final database contains 2,633 images of one or several ladybird beetles corresponding to photos reported by users to the *iNaturalist project* without any format restriction. Therefore there are images from different angles, focal points, and perspectives. Beetle specimens within the images have different sizes and colors, not only because of the beetle species but also due to the quality of the picture itself. Images were reported in the Joint Photographic (Experts) Group (JPG/JPEG) or Portable Graphics Format (PNG) formats, and images were also reported in various sizes.

2.2   Ladybird Beetle Detector

The detector is based on the method developed in [18] and previously adapted to detect ladybird beetle samples in [24], which does not require the use of bounding boxes or region proposals for ladybird beetle detection. It provides the location and number of detected ladybird beetles in the images using the WHD based-loss function with a fully FCNN architecture. This mechanism could be used widely as long as the output probabilistic map has the same size as the input image.

Since the WHD aims to compute the distance between two sets of points, all the pixel coordinates in an image constitute a discretized and bounded region in the Ω domain. Thus, let p_x be a scalar-value in the range $[0 \dots 1]$ that has been outputted from the FCNN at the x coordinate, and Y the corresponding predicted heat map. The WHD between p and Y is calculated by:

$$
\begin{aligned}
WHD_{(p,Y)} = {} & \frac{1}{S+\epsilon} \sum_{x \in \Omega} p_x \min_{y \in Y} d(x,y) \\
& + \frac{1}{|Y|} \sum_{y \in Y} M_\alpha[p_x d(x,y) + (1-p_x)d_{max}]
\end{aligned} \tag{1}
$$

subject to

$$
S = \sum_{x \in \Omega} p_x, \tag{2}
$$

and

$$
M_\alpha_{a \in A}[f(a)] = \left(\frac{1}{|A|} \sum_{a \in A} f^\alpha(a) \right)^{\frac{1}{\alpha}} \tag{3}
$$

where x and y are pixel coordinates, p_x is a pixel value of the ladybird beetle likelihood in the Ω domain, $d(\cdot,\cdot)$ refers to the Euclidean distance, and α is a similarity coefficient between the WHD and the former average Hausdorff distance. The more negative α is, the more similarity in performance between both distances.

The WHD in (1) is minimized to pinpoint the central location of the desired ladybird beetle. Thus, the ϵ coefficient in the denominator of the first term is a small positive number that provides stability if the model fails to detect the objects [4], i.e. 10^{-6} when S is approximating to 0. The first term in (1) avoids estimating regions that are far from the ground truth points. On the other hand, the second term works in approximating the minimum using the generalized mean given by (3) as it can decide through p_x whether an estimated point is relevant for the loss sum. Moreover, (3) will ignore the location if $p_x = 0$ and penalize it by d_{max}, then lower activations near ground truth points are penalized. Since p does not need to be normalized, it is not applicable the unitary constraint $(S = 1)$ in (3). Finally, the output of the FCNN model is a saliency map p containing the ladybird beetle object within the image.

2.3 Experimental Setup

Data Preparation: All images in the database were converted to JPG file format and down-scaled to [256 × 256] pixels. Thus, any ladybird beetle in the image will keep their relative location. Moreover, we carried out the corresponding ground truth selection on all images, which consisted of manually selecting an inner single point at the ladybird beetle body (close as possible to the center) of each ladybird beetle available within the image as a positive class label. These tasks were mandatory to prepare the images to meet the required settings of the learning process in the training step.

Training and Test Sets: The stratified 10-fold cross-validation method [11] was applied before the classification step to build separate training and test sets in order to ensure an adequate sample ratio for all folds. Thus, the ladybird beetle detector was trained on different training sets to learn from different input space representations. Testing the detector on these different sets boosts reliable classification results for individual samples. During training, the loss function of individual models is tested using 10% of the unused images for training. Each of these validations occurred every five batches. The reliability of the test is based on reducing the loss function at every validation step.

Detector Configuration: The architecture used was U-Net, with ReLU as activation function, the convolutions were implemented as unpadded [21]. For general purposes, every pooling step has a dropout of 0.5. The original model also did not use batch normalization layers. However, large input tiles were used to reduce the batch to a single image.

The hyperparameters were used following the point estimation pipeline proposed in [18]. Thus, for all the convolutional layers, the kernel size was set to [3 × 3]. The max-pooling kernel size used a [2 × 2] dimension with a stride of 2 units in the contracting path. The model started with 64 channels and used 512 channels in the last 5 layers. For the expansive path, bilinear upsamplig with a stride of 2 is used while concatenating it with the equivalent downsampling map. The learning rate was set to 1×10^{-4}. The number of iterations (epochs) varied from 50 to 1,000 with increment steps of 10 units and a batch size of 64 units. Finally, the detector used the SGD (stochastic gradient descent) optimizer.

Furthermore, the loss function in the WHD method (Euclidean distance by default) was optimized using four different distance equations. Thus, the distance function $d(\cdot, \cdot)$ in (1) were changed to:

- Chebyshev distance [19]: this metric is defined as the maximum positive value of the coordinate difference of the location of two elements/objects. This distance is calculated as:

$$d_{(x,y)} = \max_{i=1}^{m} |x_i - y_i|$$

- Manhattan distance [19]: this metric sums all positive coordinate differences of the location of two objects/elements. This metric is computed as:

$$d_{(x,y)} = \sum_{i=1}^{m} |x_i - y_i|$$

- Mahalanobis distance [6]: this metric allows measure the distance between two coordinate vectors, taking into account the correlation between them. Expressed by the covariance matrix Σ, it is formulated as:

$$d_{(x,y)} = \sqrt{(x-y)\Sigma^{-1}(x-y)^T}$$

- Canberra distance [19]: this metric corresponds to a weighted sum of the absolute value of the coordinate differences of two elements divided by the sum of their corresponding coordinate absolute values. This metric is calculated as:

$$d_{(x,y)} = \sum_{i=1}^{m} \frac{|x_i - y_i|}{|x_i| + |y_i|}$$

In general, x and y variables for all equations refer to $m-$dimensional vectors.

Validation Metrics: We calculated the mean and standard deviation of accuracy (ACC), precision (PRE), recall (REC), and F1-score to assess the effectiveness of the employed ladybird beetle detector on the experimental database over 10 runs. These metrics allow us to determine whether or not the detection performance is reasonable and if there is any evidence of overfitting during the training phase of the detector.

The implementation of the detector was made in Python language version 3.6.9 [14] with *scikit-learn (SKlearn)* and Keras [5] libraries.

3 Results and Discussion

According to the experimental setup, the performance evaluation of the ladybird beetle detector on a database with 2,633 images taken in random environments highlighted successful results, as shown in Table 1.

Table 1. Performance results of the ladybird beetle detector using 10 fold cross-validation.

Distances	ACC[a]	PRE[a]	REC[a]	F1-score[a]
Euclidean (default) [18]	89.40 ± 0.24	94.91 ± 0.84	85.36 ± 0.95	92.07 ± 0.52
Chebyshev [19]	90.74 ± 1.00	98.26 ± 0.35	89.48 ± 1.25	94.36 ± 0.60
Manhattan [19]	90.77 ± 1.17	94.96 ± 0.04	86.70 ± 1.14	92.81 ± 0.63
Mahalanobis [6]	67.64 ± 1.80	83.98 ± 0.47	60.65 ± 1.30	74.91 ± 0.94
Canberra [19]	49.11 ± 6.25	77.00 ± 5.52	43.90 ± 6.66	60.00 ± 6.36

[a]All values are expressed in percent and represent the mean and standard deviation of the metrics.

3.1 Performance Evaluation

From Table 1, it is possible to read the excellent performance of the FCNN-based detector using different distance functions. At least for the Euclidean, Chebyshev, and Manhattan distances, it was able to obtain a mean of detection over the 89% for all validation metrics. Similar successful results were not observed for the Mahalanobis and Canberra distances, which revealed the worst detection performance on almost all the assessment metrics. Except in the precision metric, the two later distance functions reached scores around 80%.

Notably, the Manhattan distance obtained the best precision score (PRE = 90.77 ± 1.17) while Chebyshev dominated the remaining metrics. These results are linked to the nature of each distance in the process of reducing the cost function in (1) to determine the closer the estimated points by the FCNN model are to the ground truth points. The Euclidean distance measures the shortest distance to go from one point to another, and Manhattan is the sum of the absolute difference of the components of the vectors. Both metrics try to estimate the points closer to the ground truth but limit the reduction process of the cost function. In contrast, the Chebyshev distance is the greatest of the differences along any coordinate dimension of two vectors. That enables substantial space for minimizing the cost function. Thus, to improve the ladybird beetle detection (see Table 1).

Regarding the detector learning process, it is possible to state that it was successfully trained without overfitting only for three out of five employed distance functions in the WDH, as confirmed by the trajectory of the training and validation curves shown in Fig. 1. From this figure, it is reasonable to notice that the Euclidean, Chebyshev, and Manhattan distances provided smooth and near curves during the training and validation steps as a signal of quality learning. Conversely, the behavior of the curves of the Mahalanobis and Canberra distances are separated and exhibited abrupt changes on every single epoch, proving an unsuccessful model training.

Concerning the detection heat map, it is worth mentioning that it helps visualize which regions of an image the network believes a ladybird beetle can be found. A heat map is created using high activation points proximate to the pixel estimation over the ladybird beetle. In this sense, the activation points decide if any close pixel is "ladybird enough" to trace the heat map. Successful detections will have a heat map resembling a ladybird beetle figure, and that

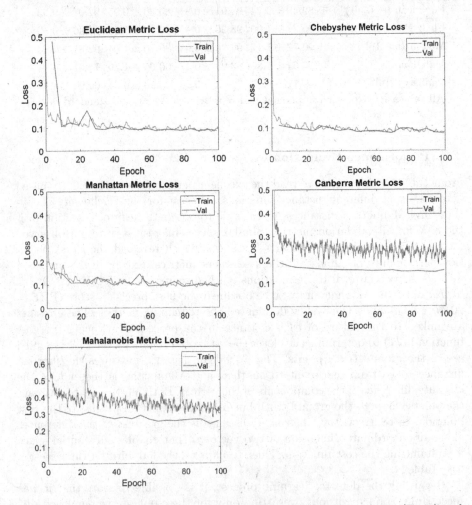

Fig. 1. Loss performance based on the WHD during the model training (Train) and validation (Val). From left to right and top to bottom, the Euclidean (default) [18], Chebyshev [19], Manhattan [19], Canberra [19], and Mahalanobis [6] distances.

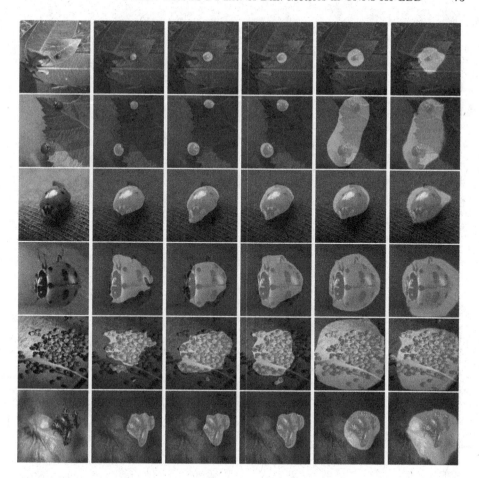

Fig. 2. Examples of successful ladybird beetle detection using the implemented method. From left to right, the original image, the result obtained with the Euclidean (default) [18], Chebyshev [19], Manhattan [19], Mahalanobis [6], and Canberra [19] distances.

was mostly achieved in the presence of small ladybird beetles in the images, as shown in Fig. 2, rows 1 and 2. On the other hand, unsuccessful detections provide a heat map matching a random figure, which often occurs in the presence of big ladybird beetles in the images, as shown in Fig. 2, rows 3 and 4. These effects are based on the heat map approach, which is prone to produce wrong detections when the ladybird beetle and its surrounding elements contain similar features.

The FCNN-based detector with the WHD using the Euclidean, Chebyshev, and Manhattan distances detected most of the ladybird beetles despite their size, number, or color variation. It generated and estimated heat maps that surround most of the ladybird beetles in the images, demonstrating a successful detection performance, as shown in Fig. 2, columns 2, 3, and 4. However, when it used the

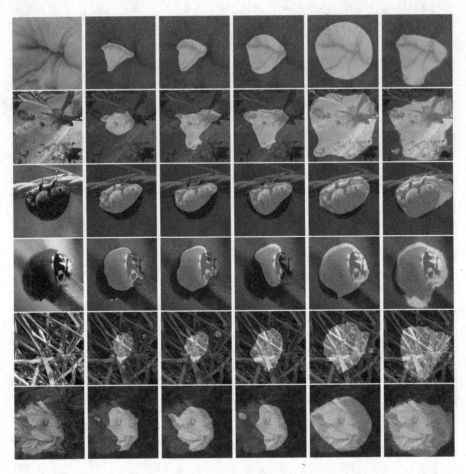

Fig. 3. Examples of unsuccessful performance of the method: From left to right, the original image, the result obtained with the Euclidean (default) [18], Chebyshev [19], Manhattan [19], Mahalanobis [6], and Canberra [19] distances.

Mahalanobis and Canberra distances, the heat map was spread over the ladybird beetles. Still, it never detected them satisfactorily, as shown in Fig. 2, columns 5 and 6. In the presence of multiple ladybirds in an image, Fig. 2 rows 2, 5, and 6, Euclidean, Chebyshev, and Manhattan performed well when few ladybirds can be spotted separately and underestimated or surrounded the region occupied by ladybirds in the presence of many (sometime overlapped). For Mahalanobis and Canberra no matter the quantity of ladybirds in the image, both metrics overestimated the region occupied by ladybirds.

Model drawbacks rely mostly on pictures where homogeneous features exist near ladybird beetles, making the models overestimate the size of a ladybird beetle or selecting those features as one. This would happen mostly when a ladybird beetle is close to a flower, hand, or another object with similar characteristics

(Fig. 3 rows 1 and 2). Another problem in the model is that the heat map can sometimes enclose just a fraction of the ladybird beetle body. For instance, it will just take some features and mark them as an object. This occurs mainly in images where the ladybird beetle appears to be larger or badly illuminated. However, this does not seems to be a drawback for the Mahalanobis metric (Fig. 3 rows 4 and 6). The fact that in the presence of many objects of the same kind, the method is not able to recognize them individually is a known drawback of the Ribera et al. [18] method. Nevertheless, this is not an issue in our case since the regions marked with more than one ladybird beetle are where they are.

4   Conclusions and Future Work

Although previous work has been developed to detect and classify beetles (ladybird beetles included) [1,23]. Detecting ladybird beetles in natural scenarios (like those provided by the *iNaturalist* project) remains a difficult task and further research is needed.

We analyzed one object detection method (originally used to pinpoint the exact location of objects in an image and count them). We applied it for ladybird beetle detection with satisfactory results. This model relies on minimizing the WHD-based loss function in an FCNN where the metric used by default is the Euclidean distance. We trained several models varying the metric used in the WHD-based loss function using Chebyshev, Manhattan, Mahalanobis, and Canberra distances. The models using Chebyshev, Manhattan, and Euclidean distances could detect almost all ladybird beetles without incurring problems such as pointing other objects as ladybird beetles or mistakenly addressing ladybird beetle figures. The model using Chebyshev distance achieved high scores of 90.74% in accuracy, precision of 98.26%, recall of 89.48%, and F1-score of 94.36%. This model outperformed those models using Euclidean, Manhattan, Mahalanobis, and Canberra distances. Chebyshev distance as part of the WHD-based loss function in FCNN provides better results for ladybird detection.

Regarding the novelty of the method used, it is important to highlight that using pixel locations and not bounding boxes (which are time-consuming, harder to draw, and in the presence of several objects tend to overlap) as ground truth makes supervised training models easier since there are substantial time savings while tagging images.

Future work includes using perceptually uniform sequential color maps to define better the location of a possible ladybird beetle and the estimated heat map for ladybird beetle classification. Also, to follow the original intention of this model, we plan to improve training with data augmentation using images with more than one ladybird beetle present. Moreover, last but not least, we plan to explore the effect of using different hyperparameters (while training) to achieve fine-tuned models.

Acknowledgment. Authors would like to thank Emilia Peñaherrera for helping in the revision of the *iNaturalist* database. The Applied Signal Processing and Machine Learning Research Group of Universidad San Francisco de Quito (USFQ) provided the computing infrastructure (iMac Pro and NVidia DGX workstations) to implement and execute the developed source code.

References

1. Abeywardhana, D., Dangalle, C., Nugaliyadde, A., Mallawarachchi, Y.: Deep learning approach to classify Tiger beetles of Sri Lanka. Eco. Inform. **62**, 101286 (2021)
2. Boenisch, F., Rosemann, B., Wild, B., Wario, F., Dormagen, D., Landgraf, T.: Tracking all members of a honey bee colony over their lifetime. arXiv preprint arXiv:1802.03192 (2018)
3. Brown, P.M., Thomas, C.E., Lombaert, E., Jeffries, D.L., Estoup, A., Handley, L.J.L.: The global spread of Harmonia axyridis (Coleoptera: Coccinellidae): distribution, dispersal and routes of invasion. Biocontrol **56**(4), 623–641 (2011). https://doi.org/10.1007/s10526-011-9379-1
4. Cai, E., Baireddy, S., Yang, C., Crawford, M., Delp, E.J.: Deep transfer learning for plant center localization. In: Proceedings of the IEEE/CVF Conference on Computer Vision and Pattern Recognition Workshops, pp. 62–63 (2020)
5. Chollet, F., et al.: Keras (2015). https://keras.io
6. De Maesschalck, R., Jouan-Rimbaud, D., Massart, D.L.: The Mahalanobis distance. Chemom. Intell. Lab. Syst. **50**(1), 1–18 (2000)
7. Girshick, R.: Fast R-CNN. In: Proceedings of the IEEE International Conference on Computer Vision, pp. 1440–1448 (2015)
8. González, G., Hanley, G.A., Gordon, R.D.: South American Coccinellidae (Coleoptera), part xix: Overview of cryptognathini and systematic revision of South American Cryptognatha Mulsant (2019)
9. Hodek, I., Evans, E.W.: Food Relationships, Chap. 5, pp. 141–274. Wiley, New York (2012). https://doi.org/10.1002/9781118223208.ch5
10. Høye, T.T., et al.: Deep learning and computer vision will transform entomology. Proc. Natl. Acad. Sci. **118**(2), e2002545117 (2021)
11. López, F.G., Torres, M.G., Batista, B.M., Pérez, J.A.M., Moreno-Vega, J.M.: Solving feature subset selection problem by a parallel scatter search. Eur. J. Oper. Res. **169**(2), 477–489 (2006)
12. Majerus, M.E.: A Natural History of Ladybird Beetles. Cambridge University Press, Cambridge (2016)
13. Marshall, S.A.: Beetles: The Natural History and Diversity of Coleoptera. Firefly Books Richmond Hillm, Ontario (2018)
14. Python Core Team: Python 3.6.9: A dynamic, open source programming language. Python Software Foundation (2019). https://www.python.org/
15. Ratnayake, M.N., Dyer, A.G., Dorin, A.: Tracking individual honeybees among wildflower clusters with computer vision-facilitated pollinator monitoring. PLoS ONE **16**(2), e0239504 (2021)
16. Redmon, J., Divvala, S., Girshick, R., Farhadi, A.: You only look once: unified, real-time object detection. In: Proceedings of the IEEE Conference on Computer Vision and Pattern Recognition, pp. 779–788 (2016)
17. Respondek, J., Westwańska, W.: Counting instances of objects specified by vague locations using neural networks on example of honey bees. Annals Comput. Sci. Inf. Syst. **18**, 87–90 (2019)

18. Ribera, J., Guera, D., Chen, Y., Delp, E.J.: Locating objects without bounding boxes. In: Proceedings of the IEEE/CVF Conference on Computer Vision and Pattern Recognition, pp. 6479–6489 (2019)
19. Rodrigues, É.O.: Combining Minkowski and Cheyshev: new distance proposal and survey of distance metrics using K-nearest neighbours classifier. Pattern Recogn. Lett. **110**, 66–71 (2018)
20. Rodríguez, I., Branson, K., Acuña, E., Agosto-Rivera, J., Giray, T., Mégret, R.: Honeybee detection and pose estimation using convolutional neural networks. Congrès Reconnaissance des Formes, Image, Apprentissage et Perception (RFIAP) (2018)
21. Ronneberger, O., Fischer, P., Brox, T.: U-Net: convolutional networks for biomedical image segmentation. In: Navab, N., Hornegger, J., Wells, W.M., Frangi, A.F. (eds.) MICCAI 2015. LNCS, vol. 9351, pp. 234–241. Springer, Cham (2015). https://doi.org/10.1007/978-3-319-24574-4_28
22. Sledevič, T.: The application of convolutional neural network for pollen bearing bee classification. In: 2018 IEEE 6th Workshop on Advances in Information, Electronic and Electrical Engineering (AIEEE), pp. 1–4. IEEE (2018)
23. Valan, M.: Automated image-based taxon identification using deep learning and citizen-science contributions. Ph.D. thesis, Department of Zoology, Stockholm University (2021)
24. Vega, M., Benítez, D.S., Pérez, N., Riofrío, D., Ramón, G., Cisneros-Heredia, D.: Coccinellidae beetle specimen detection using convolutional neural networks. In: 2021 IEEE Colombian Conference on Applications of Computational Intelligence (ColCACI), pp. 1–5. IEEE (2021). https://doi.org/10.1109/ColCACI52978.2021.9469588
25. Venegas, P., et al.: Automatic ladybird beetle detection using deep-learning models. PLoS ONE **16**(6), e0253027 (2021). https://doi.org/10.1371/journal.pone.0253027
26. Wägele, H., et al.: The taxonomist-an endangered race. A practical proposal for its survival. Front. Zool. **8**(1), 1–7 (2011). https://doi.org/10.1186/1742-9994-8-25

Non-linear PCA for Feature Extraction in Extreme Precipitation Events Using Remote Sensing Information

Cristhian E. Fernández-Álvarez[ID] and Wilfredo Alfonso-Morales[✉][ID]

School of Electrical and Electronic Engineering, Universidad del Valle,
Santiago de Cali, Colombia
{cristhian.fernandez,wilfredo.alfonso}@correounivalle.edu.co

Abstract. This work presents a study about extreme rainfall events in Colombia southwestern between 1983 and 2019 using satellite information from CHIRPS. The information allows getting the standardized precipitation index (SPI) for four-time scales: monthly, trimestral, semestral, and annual, which is necessary to understand how spatiotemporally is wet or drought a place. Due to a large amount of data, we used a dimensional reduction approach based on neural networks knows as Non-Linear PCA to get the principal components for each scale and make five clustering procedures to identify regions with similarities. We choose the number of clusters from different clustering metrics. Although for SPI1 and SPI3, the results were inconsistent, the results for SPI6 y SPI12 were quite good. The SPI6 got two regions: West and East, while the SPI12 got five regions: Pacific South, Pacific North, Andean, Andean foothills, and Amazon Regions. The findings also show differences in frequency, duration, and intensity of extreme events. Thus, we conclude that for SPI6, the East region is more drought than the West one, and for SPI12, the Andean region is the driest while the Pacific South is the wettest.

Keywords: SPI · NLPCA · CHIRPS · Clustering · Deep learning · Machine learning

1 Introduction

Global warming and climate change have raised relevant questions among scientists, decision-makers and people around the World [24]. These changes are associated with a series of extreme hydro-meteorological events that generate alterations in human life and health, water and food supplies, ecosystems, and infrastructure that affect not only the economy but also affect the population [4].

Wet is associated with a continuous period of intense rainfall [5], while drought is perceived as prolonged and regionally extensive occurrences of low-average natural water availability. According to [14,21], drought can be characterized by its

© Springer Nature Switzerland AG 2022
A. D. Orjuela-Cañón et al. (Eds.): ColCACI 2021, CCIS 1471, pp. 78–92, 2022.
https://doi.org/10.1007/978-3-030-91308-3_6

onset, duration, severity (magnitude or intensity), termination, and spatial extension. Several indices have been proposed to assess drought/wet conditions, each
with its strengths and weaknesses, such as the Palmer drought severity index
(PDSI), the crop moisture index (CMI), or the standardized precipitation index
(SPI). The latter, proposed by [11], is based on the standardization of precipitation and is defined as the number of standard deviations that cumulative precipitation deviations from average conditions. The calculation and advantages of the
SPI index have been described extensively in [8,9,11,21].

Precipitation data are required as inputs to calculate such indices. They
are acquired from discrete networks such as satellite data or weather stations.
Traditionally, drought indices are calculated using *on-site* weather observations;
however, these are often scattered and unevenly distributed and may not even
be available in some isolated areas. Precipitation remote sensing products can
compensate this lack of data such as was validated in [16,25].

In [16], the CHIRPS database (Climate Hazards Group InfraRed Precipitation with Station data) was evaluated and validated in southwestern of Colombia. The database is available with a spatial resolution of $0.05^\sim$ ($\sim$5.3 km), on a
daily, pentadal, decadal, and monthly time scale [6], with excellent performance
for many countries and regions. However, handling a large amount of data is
also challenging. The amount of data requires clustering methods to achieve a
regional characterization of drought/wet conditions based on point rainfall data
[5]. Drought/wet conditions vary significantly between regions due to local and
large-scale effects [19].

Identifying homogeneous regions within a study area with different hydro-
meteorological behaviors is of particular interest for a more efficient water
resource management [5]. However, this cluster analysis using SPI is complex
due to dynamism and nonlinearity at spatial and temporal scales [15]. Therefore, it is necessary to implement data dimensionality reduction methods such
as non-linear PCA (NLPCA) and use various clustering methods that allow
identifying better regions.

Taking as a starting point the work in [16], which studied the southwest of
Colombia, specifically the department of Nariño. This work aims to regionalize
its SPI through various clustering methods to identify homogeneous regions and
characterize them based on the behavior of extreme events and drought/wet
conditions, using remote sensing precipitation data provided by CHIRPS. The
department of Nariño has an economy based on agricultural activities that, due
to the topographic and hydrographic conditions [7], in most cases depends on
rainfed agriculture[1]. This work seeks to support decision-making by identifying
regions with drought and wet characteristics that will guide the propose public
policies for the department to manage and mitigate risk to face such events.

---

[1] Agricultural activity in which humans do not contribute to soil irrigation, but use
only that which comes from rainfall.

2 Methodology

2.1 Study Area

The department of Nariño is located in the southwest of Colombia between $0°$ $21°$ and $2°$ $40°$ north latitude and $76°$ $50°$ and $79°$ $02°$ west longitude. The study area is located in northern South America and has a total area of $33,268$ km^2. It is bordered on the west by the Pacific Ocean, on the east by the Amazon rainforest, and the Andean mountains cross it from south to north on the eastern side (Fig. 1).

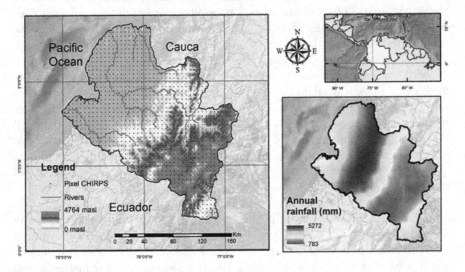

Fig. 1. Geographic location, topographic and spatial distribution of precipitation data in southwestern Colombia.

Rainfall in the department has been extensively studied in recent years. In [1], it was divided into the Pacific (West) and Andean (East) regions using 46 pluviometric stations. The seasonal rainfall regime is monomodal and bimodal for the Pacific and Andean regions, respectively [23]. In terms of spatial distribution: the Andean Region receives less rainfall with 800 mm $\cdot year^{-1}$, and in the Pacific Region a core rainfall of 7000 mm $\cdot year^{-1}$ [3]. In this work, precipitation data were used to study drought/wet events in southwestern Colombia, using CHIRPS, which was validated in [16]. CHIRPS is distributed in the study area using $1,016$ pixels, as shown in Fig. 1; each point in the figure represents a CHIRPS centroid that can be considered as an artificial station. This database has daily, pentadal, decadal, and monthly time-resolved records with a spatial resolution of $0.05°$ (~5.3 km) and near-global coverage (within $50°S$, $50°N$, $180°W$ y $180°E$) from 1981 to present.

2.2 SPI Estimation

The standardized precipitation index (SPI) is designed to quantify the deficit or excess of precipitation in a region in different time scales. The SPI is calculated from precipitation records (ideally continuous periods between 20 and 30 years of monthly values) [17]. These records can be grouped in different time scales, usually 3, 6, and 12 months, which allow the analysis of different types of drought. Meteorological and soil moisture conditions respond to precipitation anomalies on short time scales (between 1 and 6 months), while river flows, reservoir storage, and groundwater respond to long-term precipitation anomalies (6 months and up to 24 months or more).

Monthly precipitation data from CHIRPS were grouped into four scaled cumulative precipitation series: monthly (SPI1), quarterly (SPI3), semiannual (SPI6), and annual (SPI12), which were constructed from a moving sum and fitted to the distribution density function *gamma* as recommended in [12]. The density function was then transformed to a standardized normal distribution. This transformation of monthly rainfall is four times series for each pixel (1,016 pixels × 4-time series). A central feature of SPI is to allow drought monitoring with normalization of precipitation with a mean of 0 and a standard deviation of 1. Negative values less than or equal to -1.0 represent droughts, and positive values greater than or equal to 1.0 indicates that precipitation has been above the historical mean. Table 1 shows the proposed classification in [17].

Table 1. Drought classification by SPI. Adapted from [11].

SPI value	Category
2.0 or more	Extremely wet
1.5 to 1.99	Severely wet
1.0 to 1.49	Moderately wet
0.99 to -0.99	Normal
-1.0 to -1.49	Moderately drought
-1.5 to -1.99	Severely drought
-2.0 or less	Extremely drought

2.3 Non-linear PCA (NLPCA)

NLPCA is based on a *feedforward* neural network with a self-associative topology, also known as *deep-autoencoder*. NLPCA is a non-linear generalization of the classical PCA method that seeks to overcome the limitations of PCA when involving non-linear processes [13]. This topology performs an identity mapping, where the training process seeks to make the inputs (X) and outputs ($\hat{X}$) of the network the same. Figure 2 shows the NLPCA architecture, where the encoding and decoding stages are observed, the latent layer (z_1) indicates the number of principal non-linear components (NLPCs) of this type of architecture.

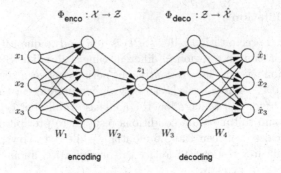

Fig. 2. NLPCA neural network topology. Adapted from [22].

This method successfully reduces dimensionality and creates a spatial map of features similar to the actual distribution of the underlying system parameters [2]. In other words, NLPCA helps to establish the dominant modes of variability in the data [2]. Details about the model are available in [22] and [10]. Using the SPI indices at different time scales, dimensionality reduction was performed for each data set through the toolbox[2] of Matlab provided in [22].

2.4   Clustering Methods and Validation Metrics

Clustering methods are used to identify data with similar characteristics. Using the NLPCs resulting from processing the SPI, five clustering methods were used, these were *SOM* (Kohonen Self-Organizing Maps), HC_{div} (Hierarchical Divisive), HC_{aglo} (Hierarchical Agglomerative), *Fuzzy C-Means* and *Kmeans*. Details on these methods are described in [18].

3   Results

3.1   Non-linear Principal Components (NLPCs)

The way to evaluate the performance of the training process of this network topology is by observing the explained variance of each NLPCs for different topologies. The selection of the number of NLPCs (latent layer) was based on the PCA, selecting the number of eigenvalues more significant or higher than one [1, 20]. A training set with SPI data for different time scales was performed to evaluate the performance and compare the results obtained using the linear principal component analysis method (PCA) and the non-linear method (NLPCA).

Table 2 shows the PCA results where the first principal component (PC1) explains a variance above 50% for all cases, the second component (PC2) explains a variance above the 10% and the sum of the explained variance of the first five principal components is above 80%.

---

[2] Toolbox available at: http://www.nlpca.org.

Table 2. Calculation of PCA for SPI data on different time scales.

Data	Variance explained (%)				
	PC1	PC2	PC3	PC4	PC5
SPI1	57.176	19.835	6.448	3.131	2.219
SPI3	54.044	21.334	7.567	3.419	2.577
SPI6	52.559	23.215	8.044	4.197	2.504
SPI12	53.717	22.724	8.601	4.958	2.136

To calculate the NLPCs, a training set was performed, reaching a total of 120 registers. Table 3 consolidates the best results obtained for a 444-200-20-5-20-200-444 topology where the input and output layer (444) represents the number of months in the study period. The values in the table describe the explained variance achieved, where the first two components (NLPC1 and NLPC2) explain more than 88% at all scales.

Table 3. Calculation of NLPCA for SPI data on different time scales.

Data	Variance explained (%)				
	NLPC1	NLPC2	NLPC3	NLPC4	NLPC5
SPI1	76.188	12.982	2.045	0.160	0.043
SPI3	74.476	13.485	1.218	0.645	0.341
SPI6	77.867	13.371	1.437	0.834	0.283
SPI12	78.128	19.000	1.484	0.543	0.351

From the previous results, NLPCA has a more significant explained variance than those obtained using PCA. The first linear component (PC1) in its best-explained variance is 57.176%; the explained variance is less than the variance of NLPC1 for all cases. In addition, the sum of the explained variance of the first five principal components for the linear and non-linear method results in an explained variance of 80% and 88%, respectively, a result that confirms that NLPCA has a more significant explained variance than PCA for the processed data sets.

3.2 Evaluation Metrics for Clustering and Homogeneous Region Delimitation Methods

With the reduced data, the clustering methods (SOM, HC_{div}, HC_{aglo}, $Fuzzy$ and $Kmeans$) were used and the optimal number of clusters K was evaluated by making variations of the number of clusters ($k = 2, 3, 4, 5$) in the different methods. The validation metrics used were: *Silhouette, Davies-Bouldin, Calinski-Harabasz* and *CS*. The results are shown in the radar graph for SPI1 (Fig. 3),

SPI3 (Fig. 4), SPI6 (Fig. 5) and SPI12 (Fig. 7), where each vertex represents a clustering method and the line represents the magnitude of each metric. A value of one indicates a better result.

As seen in Fig. 3 for SPI1 it is not possible to define a value of K. Similarly, the results presented for SPI3 in Fig. 4 are inconclusive.

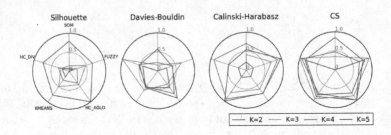

Fig. 3. Evaluation metrics for clustering methods, SPI1.

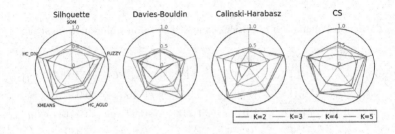

Fig. 4. Evaluation metrics for clustering methods, SPI3.

In contrast, with SPI6 and SPI12, the results were consistent. In SPI6, three indices (Silhouette, Davis-Bouldin, and CS) showed that the optimal number of clusters is $K = 2$, as shown in Fig. 5. Once the K value was defined, these regions were spatialized, as seen in Fig. 6. The obtained regions are described below.

– Region 1 or "Eastern Region", delimited in yellow, is located to the east of the study area and crosses it from south to north. This region coincides with the Andes Mountains and the Amazonian slope.
– Region 2 or "Western Region", delimited in blue, is located in the western part of the study area, covering most of the zone, including the Colombian Pacific plain and the foothills of the Pacific slope of the Andes.

According to Fig. 6 it is observed that the spatialization is consistent in almost all methods, except for HC_{aglo} which shows the larger eastern region, encompassing the southeast and northwest of the study region.

Likewise, for SPI12, the indices showed that the optimal number of clusters is $K = 5$, as shown in Fig. 7. The obtained clustering spatialization is described with the following regions.

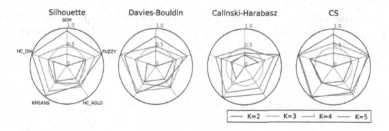

Fig. 5. Evaluation metrics for clustering methods, SPI6.

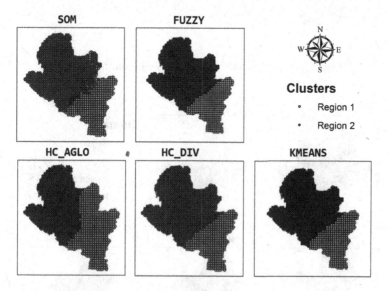

Fig. 6. Spatialization of the identified regions, SPI6.

– Region 1 or "Amazon Region", delimited in purple, is located in the southeast of the study area and coincides with the eastern flank of the Andes on the Amazon flank.
– Region 2 or "North Pacific Region", delimited in yellow, is located in the northwest of the study area with a thin line connecting north and south. The region is located in the flat area of the Colombian Pacific flank.
– Region 3 or "South Pacific Region", delimited in pink, is located in the southeast of the study area, bordering the neighboring country of Ecuador, the Pacific Ocean, and the North Pacific region.
– Region 4 or "Andean Region", delimited in orange, is located to the east of the study area, a strip covering the highest part of the Andes mountain range and crossing the study area from south to north.
– Region 5 or "Region Piedemonte Andino", delimited in blue, is located in the center of the study area and crosses it from south to north as a strip parallel to the Andean Region. This region coincides with the topographic transition

between the lowest part of the study area (Pacific Basin - Southern Region and Northern Pacific) to the highest part of the study area (Andes Mountains - Andean Region).

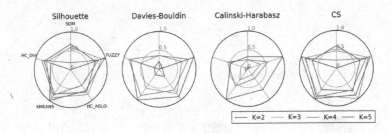

Fig. 7. Evaluation metrics for clustering methods, SPI6.

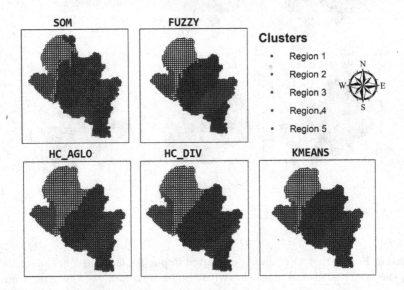

Fig. 8. Spatialization of the identified regions, SPI12.

4   Evaluation and Characterization of Each Region

4.1   Characterization of SPI6 Regions

The statistics obtained from the Eastern Region (ER), representing 70% of the study area and the Western Region (WR) representing 30%, are presented in Table 4.

Table 4. Statistics by region, SPI6.

Statistic	ER	WR
mean	42e-6	−309e-6
min	−3.91	−3.35
max	3.48	3.97
P5	−1.64	−1.59
P25	−0.66	−0.67
P50	−0.04	−0.04
P75	0.69	0.65
P95	1.66	1.71

According to the results, the drought is pervasive in the ER. The minimum value in the ER with −3.91, indicating the extreme drought event. The 5th percentile (P5) was −1.64 in ER and −1.59 in WR; this indicates that the 5% of the most negative SPI6 values have a higher magnitude in ER than in WR. The wet events are more noticeable in the WR. The maximum value in the ER is 3.49. The 95th percentile (P95) indicates a 1.71 in the WR and 1.66 in the ER, characterizing the extreme wet commonly present in the WR. The mean value is zero in both regions. In contrast, the 50th percentile (P50) shows a slight skewness of both data sets to the left, the percentiles: 25th (P25), 75th (P75) indicate very similar behavior between regions.

Table 5 presents the characteristics of drought and extreme wet events, according to the SPI6 mean value for each region (Fig. 9). Only events with a duration longer than three months are recorded since rainfed crops begin to be seriously affected after three months after the occurrence of an extreme event (these records longer than three months also apply to the Table 7)..

The occurrence of extreme events is higher in the WR with 34 events, compared to the ER with 24 events; this characteristic contrasts with the duration of the events, which is higher in the ER, as well as with the magnitude. In general terms, the ER is characterized by the predominance of drought, considering the area under the curve for negative SPI6 values of 159.94, while the area under the curve for the WR is 140.89.

Table 5. Event characteristics by region, SPI6.

Characteristics	Sign	ER	WR
Number of	SPI +	11	18
events	SPI −	13	16
Longer Duration	SPI +	29	26
(months)	SPI −	34	28
Longer	SPI +	2	2.1
magnitude	SPI −	2.2	1.7
Area under	SPI +	159.7	139.8
curve	SPI −	159.9	140.8

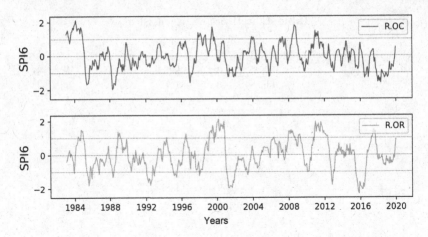

Fig. 9. Mean by region, SPI6. From top to bottom: W.R and E.R.

4.2   Characterization of SPI12 Regions

The SPI12 regions identified (Fig. 8) were five. The area occupied by each region is: Amazonian (AMR) - 18%, North Pacific (NPR) - 23%, South Pacific (SPR) - 14%, Andean (AR) - 20% and Andean piedmont (APR) - 25%. The basic statistics are presented in Table 6.

Table 6. Statistics by region, SPI12.

Statistic	AMR	NPR	SPR	AR	APR
mean	3e-6	−165e-6	−689e-6	−98e-6	−118e-6
min	−4.03	−3.03	−2.68	−3.37	−3.13
max	3.27	3.32	3.77	3.17	3.61
P5	−1.53	−1.60	−1.50	−1.56	−1.61
P25	−0.63	−0.67	−0.71	−0.68	−0.70
P50	−0.06	−0.05	−0.05	−0.10	−0.01
P75	0.67	0.65	0.52	0.70	0.65
P95	1.68	1.75	1.87	1.75	1.69

The statistics show that AR and AMR present the lowest values of SPI12 with −3.37 and −4.03, respectively. The A.R in P5 value is −1.56; this region stands out with drought characteristics associated with being the region with the lowest precipitation in the study area (see the spatial distribution of precipitation in Fig. 1).

SPR has the highest extreme wet events and a maximum humidity value of 3.77. In addition, the P95 value is 1.87, the highest compared to other regions.

NL-PCA for Feature Extraction in Extreme Precipitation Events

The Pacific region (SPR and NPR) is divided by antagonistic characteristics of extreme events analyzed; negative SPI12 is predominant in NP.R and opposite in SP.R. The division of the Pacific into south and north is present in [1] for the precipitation variable in four of the five regionalization methods analyzed. The mean values of SPI12 are close to zero and predominate in all regions; the P25, P50, and P75 values show a standard behavior without significant differentiation from one region to another.

The magnitude of the events in the five regions through the area under the curve in Fig. 10 shows that AR presents marked drought characteristics in the whole study area with a value of 184 for negative events (SPI −), being the highest in magnitude compared with other regions.

SPR has the most extreme positive (SPI +) event of 3.4. In contrast, AR has the most extreme negative event of −2.5; APR and AMR present higher frequency and lower magnitude; APR recorded 24 events in total, the highest among all regions; the low magnitude of the events compensates this frequency.

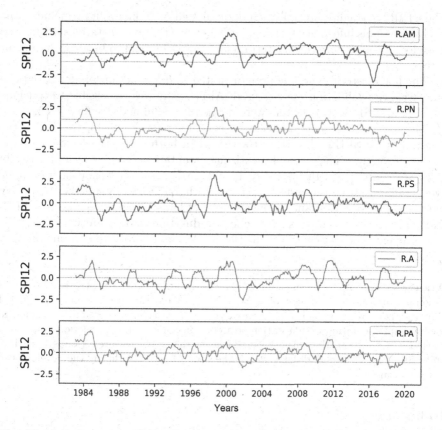

Fig. 10. Mean by region, SPI12. From top to bottom: AMR, NPR, SPR, AR y APR

Table 7. Event characteristics by region, SPI12.

Characteristics	Sign	AMR	NPR	SPR	AR	APR
Number of	SPI +	8	9	10	8	12
Events	SPI −	10	9	10	9	12
Longer Duration	SPI +	58	35	37	55	30
(months)	SPI −	45	92	31	47	55
Longer	SPI +	2.5	2.5	3.4	2.1	2.5
magnitude	SPI −	1.6	2.3	2.1	2.5	1.7
Área under	SPI +	166.1	165.9	166.3	168.5	141.8
curve	SPI −	165.8	166.2	167.2	168.8	142.5

5   Conclusions

The CHIRPS satellite precipitation data allowed us to know and regionalize the study area. This information is of great help since the *in situ* stations are limited considering the topology of the terrain and that they tend to be areas of difficult access.

The five clustering methods used resulted in different clusters for variations of k, with the validation metrics used. Although it was impossible to conclude for SPI1 and SPI3, two clusters were defined for SPI6 and five for SPI12.

The identified regions allow us to conclude that for SPI6, the ER is the driest; and for SPI12, the AR is the driest. In both cases, the region with the greatest drought events coincides with the mountainous zone, which historically has low precipitation. In SPI12, APR and AMR show the behavior of extreme events different from the rest of the regions, characterized by a higher frequency but of shorter duration and, in most cases, of lower magnitude. The AR, SPR, and NPR have the most extreme climatic duration and magnitude. The SPR has more extreme wet events, while the NPR is more prone to extreme drought events.

Acknowledgments. The authors would like to thank the Ministry of Science of Colombia and the government of Nariño for financing the research project entitled "Analysis of extreme precipitation events associated with climate variability and change for the implementation of adaptation strategies in agricultural production systems in Nariño." In addition, the authors would like to thank the research groups IREHISA and PSI of the Universidad del Valle for the support received during the development of this research.

References

1. Canchala, N.T., Ocampo-Marulanda, C., Alfonso-Morales, W., Carvajal-Escobar, Y., Ceron, W., Caicedo-Bravo, E.: Comparing methods to regionalizarion of monthly rainfall in soutwestern Colombia. Ann. Braz. Acad. Sci. (2020, in Print)

2. Canchala, T., Alfonso-Morales, W., Carvajal-Escobar, Y., Cerón, W.L., Caicedo-Bravo, E.: Monthly rainfall anomalies forecasting for southwestern Colombia using artificial neural. Water **12**(9), 2628 (2020)

3. Ceron, L.W., Andreoli, R., Toshie, K.M., Ferreria, D.S.R., Canchala, N.T., Carvajal-Escobar, Y.: Comparison of spatial interpolation methods for annual and seasonal rainfall in two hotspots of biodiversity in South America. Anais de Academia Brasileira de Ciencias (2020)

4. Corponariño WWF: Plan Territorial de Adaptación Climática del departamento de Nariño (2016). www.tulua.gov.co/wp-content/uploads/2017/07/PlanTerritorialdeSalud2016-2019.pdf

5. Espinosa, L.A., Portela, M.M., Pontes Filho, J.D., Studart, T.M.D.C., Santos, J.F., Rodrigues, R.: Jointly modeling drought characteristics with smoothed regionalized SPI series for a small island. Water **11**(12), 1–27 (2019). https://doi.org/10.3390/w11122489

6. Funk, C., et al.: The climate hazards infrared precipitation with stations - a new environmental record for monitoring extremes. Sci. Data **2**, 1–21 (2015). https://doi.org/10.1038/sdata.2015.66

7. Gobernacion de Nariño: Plan de Desarrollo Departamental Gobernación de Nariño. Plan de Desarrollo Departamental. Gobernación de Nariño, p. 255 (2016). https://sitio.narino.gov.co/

8. Guttman, N.B.: Accepting the standardized precipitation index: a calculation algorithm. J. Am. Water Resour. Assoc. **35**(2), 311–322 (1999). https://doi.org/10.1111/j.1752-1688.1999.tb03592.x

9. Hayes, M.J., Svoboda, M.D., Wilhite, D.A., Vanyarkho, O.V.: Monitoring the 1996 drought using the standardized precipitation index. Bull. Am. Meteor. Soc. **80**(3), 429–438 (1999). https://doi.org/10.1175/1520-0477(1999)080⟨0429:MTDUTS⟩2.0.CO;2

10. Hsieh, W.W.: Nonlinear principal component analysis by neural networks. Tellus Ser. A: Dyn. Meteorol. Oceanogr. **53**(5), 599–615 (2001). https://doi.org/10.3402/tellusa.v53i5.12230

11. Lloyd-Hughes, B., Saunders, M.A.: The relationship of drought frequency and duration to time sacales. Int. J. Climatol. **22**(13), 1571–1592 (2002). https://doi.org/10.1002/joc.846

12. McKee, T.B., Doesken, N.J., Kleist, J.: The relationship OD drought frecuency and duration to time scales. Int. J. Climatol. **22**(13), 1571–1592 (1993). https://doi.org/10.1002/joc.846

13. Miró, J.J., Caselles, V., Estrela, M.J.: Multiple imputation of rainfall missing data in the Iberian Mediterranean context. Atmos. Res. **197**(July), 313–330 (2017). https://doi.org/10.1016/j.atmosres.2017.07.016

14. Mishra, A.K., Singh, V.P.: A review of drought concepts. J. Hydrol. **391**(1-2), 202–216 (2010). https://doi.org/10.1016/j.jhydrol.2010.07.012

15. Nuñez Cobo, J., Verbist, K.: Atlas de sequías de América Latina y el Caribe. UNESCO Publishing (2018)

16. Ocampo-Marulanda, C., Fernández-Álvarez, C., Cerón, W., Canchala, T., Carvajal-Escobar, Y., Alfonso-Morales, W.: Spatio-temporal assessment of the hight-resolution CHIRPS rainfall dataset for Southwestern Colombia 1983–2019. J. Pure Appl. Geophys. **In evaluat** (2020)

17. OMM: Manual de indicadores e índices de sequía (2016)

18. Omran, M., Engelbrecht, A., Salman, A.: An overview of clustering methods. Intell. Data Anal. **11**, 583–605 (2007). https://doi.org/10.3233/IDA-2007-11602

19. Pereira, L., Cordery, I., Iacovides, I.: Coping with Water Scarcity: Addressing the Challenges (2009). https://doi.org/10.1007/978-1-4020-9579-5
20. Preisendorfer, R.W.: Principal component analysis in meteorology and oceanography (1988)
21. Santos, J.F., Portela, M.M., Pulido-Calvo, I.: Regional frequency analysis of droughts in Portugal. Water Resour. Manag. **25**(14), 3537–3558 (2011). https://doi.org/10.1007/s11269-011-9869-z
22. Scholz, M., Fraunholz, M., Selbig, J.: Nonlinear principal component analysis: Neural network models and applications. In: Gorban, A.N., Kégl, B., Wunsch, D.C., Zinovyev, A.Y. (eds.) Principal Manifolds for Data Visualization and Dimension Reduction. LNCSE, vol. 58, pp. 44–67. Springer, Heidelberg (2008). https://doi.org/10.1007/978-3-540-73750-6_2
23. Urrea, V., Ochoa, A., Mesa, O.: Seasonality of rainfall in Colombia. Water Resour. Res. **55**(5), 4149–4162 (2019). https://doi.org/10.1029/2018WR023316
24. WMO: Weather extremes in a Changing Climate: Hindsight on Foresight. No. 1075 (2012)
25. Wu, W., Li, Y., Luo, X., Zhang, Y., Ji, X., Li, X.: Performance evaluation of the CHIRPS precipitation dataset and its utility in drought monitoring over Yunnan Province. China. Geomat. Nat. Hazards Risk **10**(1), 2145–2162 (2019). https://doi.org/10.1080/19475705.2019.1683082

A Smart Algorithm for Traffic Lights Intersections Control in Developing Countries

Jose D. Olaya-Quiñones[✉] and Juan C. Perafan-Villota[✉] [iD]

Automatics and Electronics Department, Universidad Autonoma de Occidente, Cll 25#115-85 Km 2 Via Cali-Jamundi, Cali, Colombia
{jose.olaya,jcperafan}@uao.edu.co

Abstract. Traffic jam is a problem that directly affects the quality of life of the population in large cities. This problem exacerbates at road intersections, where obsolete traffic control systems based on a static set of rules remain in use. We propose an algorithm that improves the vehicular flow at traffic-light intersections by optimizing a dynamic allocation of times. We train our own YOLO detector using a set of images captured from traffic cameras installed at a cross-road. Furthermore, we added an attention module to our detector which outperforms the original YOLO V3 by a mAP value of 2%. We used a fuzzy control to time allocation on intersections controlled by traffic lights. The number of vehicles detected in each intersection road allowed the creation of fuzzy rules. Since, at the local level, there are few traffic cameras installed on intersections, we build a simulated environment both to train our detector system and verify the efficiency of our algorithm.

Keywords: Smart city · Traffic jam · Deep learning · Fuzzy logic · YOLO · Unit3D

1 Introduction

In 2010, the European initiative about "smart cities" [1] presented four dimensions that should develop the cities of this type; one of these dimensions was transporting. On the other hand, the World Economic Forum [9] indicated in its study that by 2040, large urban centers will double the number of vehicles. These two reports lead to deduce that the problems related to road flow tend to increase and that a possible solution to these problems could be the creation of mechanisms that allow cities to be "smarter". Indeed, in recent years, in Colombia, there has been considerable interest by the national authorities in promoting research focused on solving this type of problem. One of the main study focus is the creation of intelligent traffic light systems [14], being the intersections a key factor of study since they are critical points of vehicular concentration or traffic jams.

Intelligent traffic lights are developed under the concept of technological innovations such as the internet of things, cloud computing, big data, and the closing of the loop in the system, i.e., feedback of information to ensure control on the

© Springer Nature Switzerland AG 2022
A. D. Orjuela-Cañón et al. (Eds.): ColCACI 2021, CCIS 1471, pp. 93–106, 2022.
https://doi.org/10.1007/978-3-030-91308-3_7

system. According to [11], about one billion traffic cameras were expected to be installed globally by 2020. This fact could result in a great benefit to the development of intelligent traffic lights because it would have the feedback data from the control system, which would consist basically in the detection and counting of the number of pedestrians and vehicles present in the different areas of study. In Sect. 2, we show some of the most relevant works in the area of intelligent traffic lights.

At the local level, the number of cameras installed on approaches to the intersections is too low, resulting in insufficient reliable visual information necessary to feed the control system. As a result, in Sect. 3, we propose the creation of a simulated environment involving streets, traffic lights, traffic cameras, pedestrians, and vehicles. To this environment, we have added some realistic aspects such as illumination changes and different types of overlays (vehicle-vehicle, pedestrian-pedestrian, and vehicle-pedestrian) to create a dataset that allows us to train a robust detection system. In this context, we use YOLO (You Only Look Once) as the state-of-the-art object detector but add an attention module to improve the detection accuracy.

The output of the detection system feeds a fuzzy control system, which is responsible for making decisions regarding the times that should be assigned to each of the traffic lights present at a particular intersection. It should be noted that this simulated environment will also be used to quantify the performance of our algorithm (see Sect. 4). Finally, we conclude in Sect. 5.

2   Related Work

The last few years have seen one marked interest in the topic of smart cities, which has led a large number of researchers to focus their efforts on the four dimensions proposed in [1]. One of the big problems facing transport is the assigning of fixed times to the traffic lights. Taking into account only statistical studies about vehicular behavior generates continuous traffic congestion.

There are two broad classes of systems used by the intelligent transportation field; the former based on radio frequency techniques and the latter based on machine learning techniques. For the former, there is some relevant research: Guler et al. [2] dedicated their research by prioritizing buses at signalized intersections with single-lane using additional traffic signals called pre-signals. Wen et al. [12] developed a system based on radio frequency identification (RFID); this system calculates the maximum flow and average car speed and uses the IF-THEN rule to provide different solutions based on particular traffic situations. Yang et al. [13] present an adaptive signal control system based on a vehicle arrival prediction model, which captures the dynamic traffic system and uses the joint probability distribution function in a connected vehicle environment.

It is worth noting that, in developing countries, the lack of fully developed infrastructure has affected the growth of those techniques that need communications as v2v (vehicle to vehicle) and vehicle to infrastructure (v2i). Therefore machine learning-based techniques seem more available according to the current technology using traffic cameras which are easily adjustable to extract information relevant to the issue.

Even though the object detection field has been many years on development, it is only in recent years that the progress became remarkable. There are several deep learning algorithms-based object detection, being the most popular: Faster Region-based CNN (Faster R-CNN) [8], Single Shot Multibox Detector (SDD) [5], and You Only Look Once (YOLO) [7]. However, Srivastava et al. [10] concluded that YOLO-V3 outperforms SSD and Faster RCNN, making it the best of the three algorithms because it is the most efficient for real-time processing despite Faster R-CNN being the most accurate. To reach the best trade-off between detection accuracy and speed, Hu et al. [3], proposed an attention mechanism named Squeeze-and-Excitation (SE), which dynamically recalibrates the channel-wise feature in a network. They showed that adding this module outperforms all the baselines on four different benchmark datasets: CIFAR-100, ImageNet-1K, MS COCO, and Places365-Challenge.

Finally, for the decision support systems that implement and handle the traffic rules, there are two main types of solutions, those based on Petri's net theory and those based on fuzzy logic. The former is available in academic literature, such as the work presented by Mu et al. [6] that studied just the control problem to give preemption at emergency vehicles using time colors Petri nets. However, are the fuzzy logic controllers that provide considerable improvements in the efficiency of traffic junctions management, as was amply demonstrated in [4].

3   Methodology

A traffic lights control system based on the detection of objects using camera images is proposed (See Fig. 1).

The idea is to take pictures of each lane to be monitored in real-time, pass them through an artificial neural network previously trained for vehicle detection; for this purpose, we use YOLO V3 (You Only Look Once) and improved its performance, adding an attention module as proposed in [3]. For the allocation of times, we address a fuzzy control which will have as input the difference between the number of vehicles detected in the lane and the average of vehicles detected in all lanes, whose output will be the time that the traffic light will be green.

It should be stated that we used Unity 3d Engine to simulate our road system since it allowed us both the acquisition of dataset and to verify the control of the traffic lights system. We developed our dataset for the YOLO training, which we built using a simulated road system and LabelImg. Nevertheless, to recreate a more realistic environment, we add variations to emulate the different light changes occurring throughout the day.

The following provides the different stages of our proposal: In stage 1, we create a simulated road system in Unity 3D. At this stage, we designed a two-lane road system in both directions with eight signalized intersections (citadel), as shown in Fig. 2.

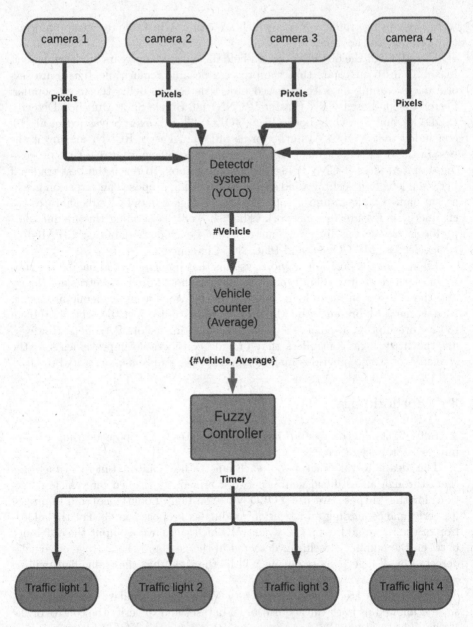

Fig. 1. System block diagram showing the logic of the whole traffic light control system.

We also added a traffic light system and, all the possibilities of trafficability were proposed for agents (vehicles and pedestrians), allowing them to choose randomly for their circulation. It's worth mentioning while there are eight intersections, the control system uses only one of them.

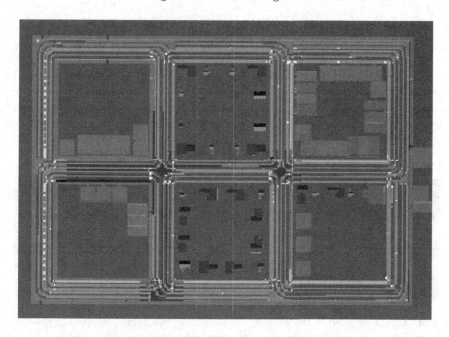

Fig. 2. Top View of our simulated city. There is a complete view of the entire citadel simulated and created in Unity 3D. Here, we conduct the corresponding tests to make the most appropriate and optimal selection of the intersection where we implemented the intelligent system.

Fig. 3. Top View showing an intersection with several lanes in different directions

Figure 3, shows the intersection selected for the system implementation, taking into account aspects such as visibility and good vehicular and pedestrian flow. We can see the waypoints as pre-recorded reference points that allow marking locations, e.g., where you are, where you are going, or where you have been.

We used the "way-point" tool provided by Unity3D to create waypoints, and we raised all possible routes where vehicles and pedestrians can travel.

We have done the vehicle's configuration through two scripts. The former is in charge of controlling speed, acceleration, and interaction with other objects. The latter is responsible for navigation, providing them with trafficability autonomy. A spawner located at a waypoint on the map generates vehicles. This spawner controlled the ratio and the vehicle number in the road system. The same is true for pedestrians (see Fig. 4).

Fig. 4. Agents involved in the project. We shown the two agents involved in the Unity 3D simulation, to the left there are some vehicles and to the right-pedestrians.

The operation of the traffic lights can raise systematically. In other words, a great system can contain a subsystem and, in turn, this can hold another subsystem. Therefore, the first system observes all the traffic-light intersections and the vehicle's and pedestrians' behavior. The first subsystem focuses on each intersection point by giving the right of way to whoever it corresponds. The second subsystem assigns time for each traffic light, as well as establishing the correct lights sequence.

For network training, we recorded twenty videos from four cameras located on intersections above the traffic lights. These videos were taken with different light angles, simulating the different positions of the sun. We converted videos into a group of images with a rate of 20 shots per minute. Lastly, we debug images with some defects. More than 2000 images were taken from the previously analyzed simulation to assign the respective labels. We define two classes to identify vehicles and persons respectively at their locations. We use a software named Labeling, which is a tool that delivers a text file containing information about the object class and the location of the box enclosing it (X1, X2, Y1, Y2).

Figure 5 shows some of the images taken in the road simulation system created in Unity3D from the different cameras used in the intersection selected for the dataset creation that will later serve as the basis for the logic program that will direct the control of the traffic lights.

In stage 3, we implemented a convolutional network based on the Darknet interface that on its website shows a comparison graph that made it easier to select the version used. We used YOLOv3 for a pre-trained network.

Fig. 5. Illustration of a sample of the second dataset performed.

After selecting YOLO V3 for the detection system, we carried out the training, which helps in detecting vehicles and pedestrians. We perform a little more than 100 epochs to reach the expected results. However, we thought we could improve the network performance, and to this end, we decided to include an attention module block named SE (Squeeze and Excitation). The main idea with this block (see Fig. 6).

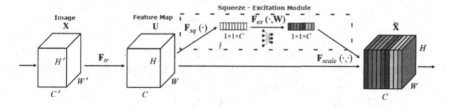

Fig. 6. Attention module Squeeze-Excitation adapted from [3]

First, they use some feature transformation, e.g., a convolution operation, over an image $\mathbf{X}(W \times H \times C')$, to get features $\mathbf{U}(W \times H \times C)$. Next, they get a single value for each canal $\mathbf{c}$ on features $\mathbf{U}$ through a squeeze operation (global average pooling), as shown in Eq. 1. After, they realize an operation (See Eq. 2) over this vector of length C to generate a new set of weights. It is important to note that this operation is the result of passing the $\mathbf{z}$ vector through two fully connected layers configured as bottleneck architecture. Finally, they obtain the output of the block by rescaling $\mathbf{U}$ with the activations $\mathbf{s}$ (See Eq. 3).

$$z_c = \mathbf{F}_{sq}(\mathbf{u}_c) = \frac{1}{H \times W} * \sum_{i=1}^{H} \sum_{j=1}^{W} u_c(i,j) \tag{1}$$

$$s = \mathbf{F}_{ex}(\mathbf{z}, \mathbf{W}) = \sigma(g(\mathbf{z}, \mathbf{W})) = \sigma(\mathbf{W}_2 \delta(\mathbf{W}_1, \mathbf{z})) \tag{2}$$

$$\tilde{x}_c = \mathbf{F}_{scale}(\mathbf{u}_c, s_c) = s_c \mathbf{u}_c \tag{3}$$

```
+------------+---------------+---------------+---------------+
| Metrics    | YOLO Layer 0  | YOLO Layer 1  | YOLO Layer 2  |
+------------+---------------+---------------+---------------+
| grid_size  | 10            | 20            | 40            |
| loss       | 0.017485      | 0.037006      | 0.037379     |
| x          | 0.004956      | 0.001075      | 0.009965     |
| y          | 0.000765      | 0.000039      | 0.009053     |
| w          | 0.000587      | 0.014066      | 0.004691     |
| h          | 0.004622      | 0.016512      | 0.008096     |
| conf       | 0.005655      | 0.005312      | 0.004189     |
| cls        | 0.000901      | 0.000003      | 0.001385     |
| cls_acc    | 100.00%       | 100.00%       | 100.00%      |
| recall50   | 1.000000      | 1.000000      | 1.000000     |
| recall75   | 1.000000      | 1.000000      | 1.000000     |
| precision  | 1.000000      | 0.666667      | 0.666667     |
| conf_obj   | 0.999201      | 0.996557      | 0.998539     |
| conf_noobj | 0.000048      | 0.000019      | 0.000027     |
+------------+---------------+---------------+---------------+
Total loss 0.09187045693397522
---- ETA 0:38:53.779136
```

Fig. 7. Illustration of the training testing process.

In the neural network training process, a testing process is performed, which provides us with information on how the training is going (see Fig. 7), showing the error and precision as the most relevant information.

Lastly, in stage 4, we designed a fuzzy control for the time allocation in the intersection with traffic lights as shown in Fig. 8.

The input to the control system is the difference between the number of vehicles detected and the average. We obtain this average with the last detection of each lane before its traffic light turns green. This calculation will give us the highest number of vehicles per lane per cycle. The linguistic rules of error statistics that we use are:

- Much more time if the error is very positive.
- High time if the error is less positive.
- Medium time if the error is medium.
- Low time if the error is negative.
- Much less time if the error is very negative.

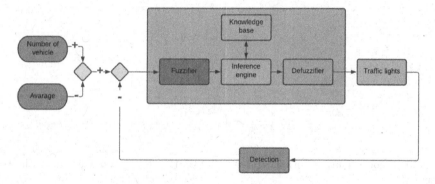

Fig. 8. A block diagram showing the operation of our fuzzy control and the handling of its inputs.

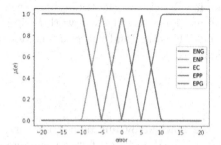

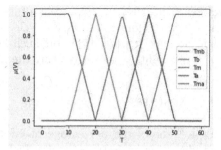

Fig. 9. Fuzzy sets of the error   **Fig. 10.** Fuzzy sets of the output

Figure 9 shows the fuzzy input set (error), which has two trapezoidal membership functions and three triangular membership functions. While in Fig. 10 is shown the fuzzy set for the output, which has the same schematic as the fuzzy input set.

For the defuzzification, we selected the centroids (See Fig. 11) because the changes are smoother and more fluid, seeing the behavior of time concerning the system error. In Fig. 12 is shown the graph of the time concerning the error using centroids, which is the fuzzy selected for the system.

Finally, Fig. 13 shows the system operation in one of its simulations, in which a possible sequence of operations is observed, taking into account the previous programming. We start from traffic light one placed in green, taking into account the vector located at the bottom of each shot which indicates detected vehicles, the times assigned to green, and yellow respectively.

Traffic light one gives way to traffic light two, which makes a jump to traffic light four because there is no detection of vehicles at traffic light three at that moment, which would be considered a time-out or wasted time. When the time at the stoplight four returns to stoplight one starting a new cycle, it goes from stoplight one to stoplight three because in the previous cycle it was not positioned

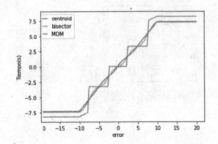

Fig. 11. Error vs Output with 3 defuzzifiers

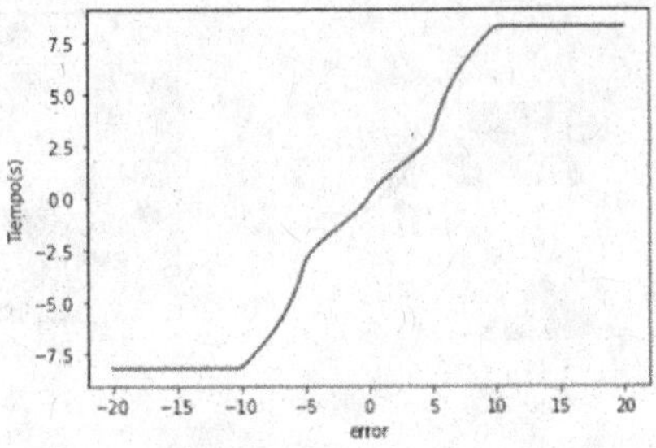

Fig. 12. Error vs Output with the selected defuzzifier (centroid)

in green. Due to this time it detects vehicles, it is given priority so that this let the circulation. After the expiration of its time, it will activate the traffic light two and then the four to fulfill this cycle, and so on. The controller will work taking into account important factors such as vehicle detection and the prioritization of traffic lights by not activating the previous cycle.

4   Results

Table 1 shows the percentage of effectiveness reached by our neural network for detecting pedestrians and vehicles. We obtained 81.92% of mean average precision (mAP) using unmodified YOLOv3, while YOLOv3 with the attention module proposed had a score of 83.5%, reflecting that the use of an attention mechanism helped raise scores of our detector. It is worth noting that the gap is greater concerning person detection.

Table 1. mAP comparison between YOLOv3 and YOLOv3 with SE Attention block.

Agents	YOLOv3	YOLOv3 + SE
Person	0.73	*0.76
Car	0.90	*0.91
mAP	81.5 %	*83.5 %

In Figs. 14 and 15, there are camera shots of the intersection, showing the capture of the objects present, marked by bounding boxes, and also identified with their respective class (car, person).

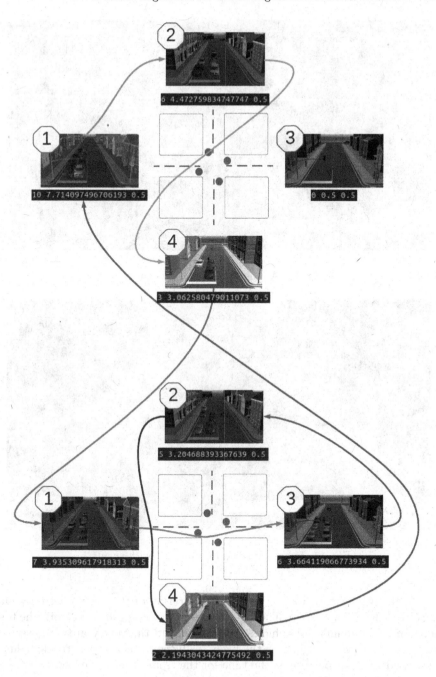

Fig. 13. Operation of the system

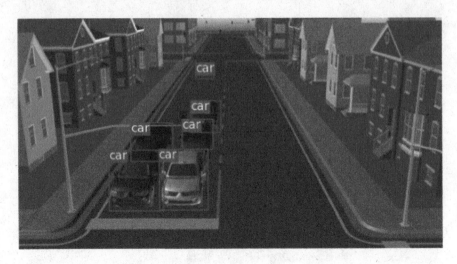

Fig. 14. An image captured by camera 3

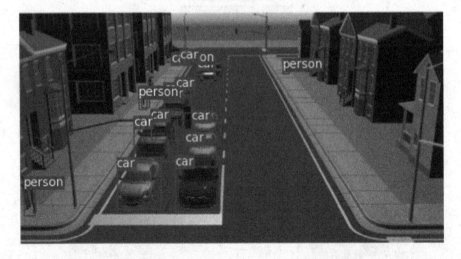

Fig. 15. Image captured by camera 1 with agents.

On the other hand, Fig. 16 shows the operation of the fuzzy controller and the object detection system. The algorithm delivers a 3-position vector. The first position is the number of vehicles detected within the yellow area, the second position is the time assigned by the fuzzy traffic controller for the traffic light in green and, the last position is the time for the traffic light in yellow.

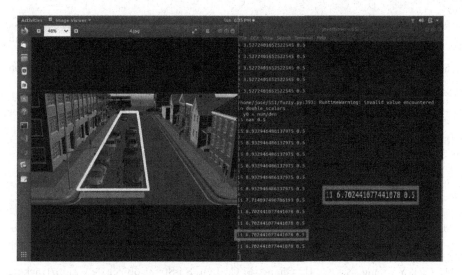

Fig. 16. Operation of fuzzy control 1 (Color figure online)

5 Conclusions

In this paper, we demonstrated that it is possible to make an intelligent controller that allows the intersections through the traffic lights to reduce the possibility of a traffic jam, which helps to optimize the time for vehicles. We also demonstrated that YOLOv3 in its version of six fps with an attention module outperforms the detection reached with the original version. The high level of accuracy and low computational cost of our detector was a key factor for this project since it depends on the capture of the agents, which is the basis for the development of the system. Furthermore, the fuzzy controller approach provides flexibility for the user since it is only necessary to modify the range of output parameters. Finally, using interconnected sensors with new technology on IoT could improve the effectiveness of this kind of architecture.

References

1. European Comission: European initiative on smart cities, 2010–2020. http://setis. ec.europa.eu/set-plan-implementation/technology-roadmaps/european-initiative-smart-cities. Accessed 9 July 2019
2. Guler, S.I., Gayah, V.V., Menendez, M.: Bus priority at signalized intersections with single-lane approaches: a novel pre-signal strategy. Transp. Res. Part C Emerg. Technol. **63**, 51–70 (2016)
3. Hu, J., Shen, L., Sun, G.: Squeeze-and-excitation networks. In: Proceedings of the IEEE Conference on Computer Vision and Pattern Recognition, pp. 7132–7141. IEEE (2018)
4. Koukol, M., Zajíčková, L., Marek, L., Tuček, P.: Fuzzy logic in traffic engineering: a review on signal control. Math. Prob. Eng. **2015** (2015)

5. Liu, W., et al.: SSD: single shot MultiBox detector. In: Leibe, B., Matas, J., Sebe, N., Welling, M. (eds.) ECCV 2016. LNCS, vol. 9905, pp. 21–37. Springer, Cham (2016). https://doi.org/10.1007/978-3-319-46448-0_2
6. Mu, H., Liu, L., Li, X.: Signal preemption control of emergency vehicles based on timed colored petri nets. Discrete Dyn. Nat. Soc. **2018** (2018)
7. Redmon, J., Divvala, S., Girshick, R., Farhadi, A.: You only look once: unified, real-time object detection. In: Proceedings of the IEEE Conference on Computer Vision and Pattern Recognition, pp. 779–788. IEEE (2016)
8. Ren, S., He, K., Girshick, R., Sun, J.: Faster R-CNN: towards real-time object detection with region proposal networks. Adv. Neural. Inf. Process. Syst. **28**, 91–99 (2015)
9. Smith, M.N.: The number of cars will double worldwide by 2040. https://www.weforum.org/agenda/2016/04/the-number-of-cars-worldwide-is-set-to-double-by-2040. Accessed 9 July 2019
10. Srivastava, S., Divekar, A.V., Anilkumar, C., Naik, I., Kulkarni, V., Pattabiraman, V.: Comparative analysis of deep learning image detection algorithms. J. Big Data **8**(1), 1–27 (2021). https://doi.org/10.1186/s40537-021-00434-w
11. Wei, Y., Song, N., Ke, L., Chang, M.C., Lyu, S.: Street object detection/tracking for AI city traffic analysis. In: 2017 IEEE SmartWorld, Ubiquitous Intelligence & Computing, Advanced & Trusted Computed, Scalable Computing & Communications, Cloud & Big Data Computing, Internet of People and Smart City Innovation (SmartWorld/SCALCOM/UIC/ATC/CBDCom/IOP/SCI), pp. 1–5. IEEE (2017)
12. Wen, W., Yang, C.L.: A dynamic and automatic traffic light control system for solving the road congestion problem. WIT Trans. Built Environ. **89** (2006)
13. Yang, L., Wang, Y., Yao, Z.: A new vehicle arrival prediction model for adaptive signal control in a connected vehicle environment. IEEE Access **8**, 112104–112112 (2020)
14. Departamento administrativo de planeación municipal - DAPM: Análisis integral de la red de infraestructura vial para la movilidad motorizada en el municipio de cali. http://idesc.cali.gov.co/download/movilidad/documento_tecnico_infraestructura_vial.pdf. Accessed 25 Oct 2019

Author Index

Printed in the United States
by Baker & Taylor Publisher Services